T0195952

MENTAL HEALTH
IN MODERN SOCIETY

Insight into Psychotherapeutic Practice

NEVENKA PODGORNIK PULEC

authorHOUSE®

AuthorHouse™ UK
1663 Liberty Drive
Bloomington, IN 47403 USA
www.authorhouse.co.uk
Phone: 0800.197.4150

Published by AuthorHouse 01/09/2019

ISBN: 978-1-7283-8326-2 (sc)
ISBN: 978-1-7283-8325-5 (e)

Print information available on the last page.

Any people depicted in stock imagery provided by Getty Images are models,
and such images are being used for illustrative purposes only.
Certain stock imagery © Getty Images.

This book is printed on acid-free paper.

Following the book

In this book, Nevenka Podgornik approaches directly and indirectly the detailed analysis of society and of an individual. Although she is focusing directly on an individual, she explains him through the social phenomena of the Western civilization, joined together by consumerism and the consumer society, which are the basic causes of the modern person's distress. She puts a mirror in front of Western civilization and the consumer society, focusing on the individual and the prevalent psychological theories, and explains what she sees in it.

In the detailed introduction, the author dissects with filigree accuracy various psychological schools by posing the question "who is a person" and confronting the answers these schools offer. She puts these answers in place alongside the connecting theory of the book and choice theory. She defines a person within the context of choice theory and she accepts him as a social, free, and responsible being, internally motivated, who intentionally uses his behaviour in order to appease his needs. She presents the concept of choice theory as a comprehensive and integrated approach to the understanding of a human personality, and also as a theoretic basis for the extremely effective reality therapy. She inserts choice theory, to which the critics frequently reproach a "non-professional" approach as compared to the prevailing theoretic psychological schools, within scientific psychology, since it belongs exactly there, thanks to the object studied, the methods, and the objectives. For this reason, the book is not only a complex scientific biography comparing choice theory to other approaches, but also a work which gives choice theory a greater potential and puts it, together with reality therapy, alongside the great schools of psychology. Within the scientific discourse the author was able to introduce just the right amount of ambition and research stubbornness to push the boundaries that limited choice theory and reality therapy until the creation of this book.

In the first two chapters, the author systematically compares choice theory with selected predominant psychological schools, which explain what an individual, society, and human spirituality are. She does not have a direct approach, but she begins this comparison by explaining the social phenomena and showing how different schools explain the late-modern society and an individual's role in it. She shows in a perceptive way how is it possible to use choice theory in explaining the social phenomena and an individual, while going a step further in understanding and in the treatment on which most of this monograph is based.

Treating mental health disorders is not a large part of the content of the monograph, but it is essential for the structure and the understanding of the content. With the help of the concept of humanistic psychology, the author shows the thorn in the side of the behaviouristic approach in understanding a person and society's functioning. At the same time, she shows why the behaviouristic approach, an individual's understanding based on external control, is the key to the functioning of the modern consumer society, oriented towards objectives and guilt.

The major part of this monograph is destined to the psychotherapeutic and socio-anthropological analysis of psychic crises. After Freud, for almost half a century, psychology was held to a biased idea that an individual is first a desperate, split, neurotic, hateful, and destructive subject. Humanistic psychology returned him the second half, a happy, loving, joyful, and optimistic half. This part of the monograph is based on the scientific research question, which affects the core of an individual in postmodern society. She does not present the phenomena, such as anxiety and uncertainty about the future, as mere consequences of social circumstances in Western society, but she treats them as consequences of an individual's active creation with an instable identity. It makes him an ideal consumer, a member of society, exigent only in appearance, and at the same time, he is completely inept and incapable of taking his life in his own hands. Despite the fact that the monograph is intended to present the treatment of mental problems in the context of an individual, the detailed analysis implicitly reflects the findings that present society's situation, which regardless of its development in the field of mental health, it got in depth as never before. The World Health Organization predicts the break and the transition from a period where in the last thirty or fifty years the main health problem was represented by coronary heart diseases. We are indeed proceeding towards a new main health challenge of the Western consumer society of wealth, and entering a period of psychic crises with reigning depression on top as a rising and at the same time ever-present basic health problem of the Western world.

The monograph shows to what point the behaviouristic view of the individual has taken us. For the holder of power or the capital manager, behaviourism, based on rewards and punishments, is an appealing system, which supposes that a human being can be externally led as a scared, frustrated and insecure individual. Sadly, behaviourism does not see that an individual's suffering is caused by his own helplessness to effectively appease his needs or transfer the frustration caused by not meeting his needs. An individual cannot, or does not know how to change most circumstances. But he can choose his behaviour in circumstances that allow him enough freedom to appease his needs. This is why the author, with a refined accuracy dissects, analyses, and studies the key relationships in order to understand an individual's present-day situation in society and plan the changes that would allow an individual to live a quality life. This society will show that existential needs are merely part of a greater field of needs in which psychic needs do not represent only an equivalent part, but a prevalent one.

In this research, Nevenka Podgornik verifies and confirms that the theoretical concepts of choice theory, on which reality therapy is based, could be used effectively in solving mental health problems. It is extremely important to underline the methodologically accurate approach that permitted the author to extract from the therapeutic materials the patterns which allowed her to verify the theoretic concepts. The value of the monograph is also presented in the fact that it summarizes the therapeutic conversations, giving students of psychology and other social sciences, and students of reality therapy and other related approaches material which could be used as teaching material and potential material for further analyses.

I am sure that the monograph will establish itself as a basic work and schoolbook for students of the psychotherapeutic school of choice theory and reality therapy, but also for all those students whose programmes include a plan for learning about and understanding a person. The monograph will find its place on bookshelves and in the hands of all those who believe it is important to understand a fellow human being – in the role of a therapist, a counsellor, or just a friend. There is another aspect which makes choice theory so specific. It is the way in which it takes away from the counsellor (therapist) the direct responsibility for the client's (patient) health and places it in the centre of the challenge, the individual. The therapist is completely responsible only for his work. The client learns to take responsibility for his choices and behaviour. This is the only way to help an individual develop into a mature, responsible, and independent person, who appeases his own needs, without getting into a conflict with himself or his social and larger circle.

A person – a being who is aware of being aware (Homo sapiens sapiens) – is a social being, who will sooner or later realize that his own well-being is linked to the well-being of a fellow human being and the well-being of all other people in a globalized society. Only then will an individual and the world start to live in the postmodern society of understanding, accepting, and wealth. Choice theory will have an important role in this process. With the present monograph, the author has added her own piece to this mosaic.

Dr. Aleksander Zadel

Contents

INTRODUCTION

The paradigmatic model of this work derives from the connection of larger humanistic sociology. The sociological discussion of contemporary social conditions in connection with mental health problems represents a problematic base for the anthropological-psychological treatment of a person.

Incertitude, instability, and vulnerability are the most common and painful characteristics of modern society as established by Bauman (2002, 202). "The phenomenon that all these concepts try to comprise and articulate is a composed experience of insecurity (condition, rights, and survival), incertitude (regarding their duration and future stability) and danger (the human body, the self, and the subsequent outgrowth of both such as: possessions, neighbourhood, community)," (ibid, 203). The transition into late modern society (Giddens) means the exclusion of an individual from traditional relations, religious systems, and social relationships; on the other hand, the pluralization of lifestyles and the competition of values aided the disintegration of relationships that give meaning to a person's life[1] (Beck, Beck-Gernsheim 2006). The risk mentioned by Beck manifests itself mostly on the level of an individual person and brings the risk within personal, intimate relationships that thus far seemed self-evident and untouchable.

According to the American psychiatrist and psychotherapist William Glasser, the disintegration of relationships is also caused by external control psychology, a term he uses for behaviours that people use in order to change other peoples' behaviours. This control mechanism is a miserable attempt to satisfy a need for power and taking control over a person and thus creating a 'disciplined society' (Foucault), which "transforms an individual into a 'case' / ... /, that we have to train or repair, classify, normalize, exclude, etc.", (Foucault 1984, 190) or to subordinate this person to a normative activity in a more subtle and indirect way by exerting a level of control over him.

The false belief that the efficacy of control and behaviours of force is connected to a basic conviction that a person is a reactive being. Personality behaviouristic theories do not

---

[1] The terms indicated in a grammatical male form are used as neutral for men and women.

concede a person's free will and free expression of emotional needs and treat people as mechanically conditioned beings. There is no consciousness, everything is conditioned by previous conditions (Pavel's conditional reflex theory, Skinner's instrumental conditioning). The theory of stimulus and reaction (classical S and R behaviourism), as an object of psychology, acknowledges only human behaviour (connections between stimuli and reactions), while ignoring the conscious action, mentality, and everything that belongs in the "black box" (Watson). The period of "the stimulus reigning" (Thurstone in Musek 2003, 17) still lasts, the mechanical S-R system is accepted "almost by everyone in the field of 'scientific' psychology, but what is more important / ... / almost every person believes it." (Glasser 2007, 39)

Fromm also has a critical view of the existing universal psychology: "The knowledge regarding a person, the psychology, which according to the great Western tradition was considered a condition for virtue, for a correct life, and happiness, degenerated into a mere tool for manipulating others and oneself, for market research, for political propaganda, advertising and so on." (Fromm 2002, 65) Fromm sees the possibilities for a complete renovation of society in the development of humanistic science regarding a person, which would steer him towards "being", towards accepting new humanistic values. He says: "The realization of a new society and a new person is possible only if old motivations, like profit and power, are replaced by new ones (living, sharing with others, understanding), if a creative and loving character manages to replace a marketing character, if the cybernetic belief is replaced by a new radical, humanistic spirit." (Fromm 2004, 180) He asks himself: "If I am what I 'have', and if I lose what I 'have', who am I?" (ibid, 83)

How to "revive" a person "alienated" from his biological essence?

The research question of this book derives from the supposition that phenomena such as risk, uncertainty, anxiety, unhappiness, and lack of connection are part of risk societies and that the modern social structure creates individuals with an unclear and unstable identity, which manifests itself in the form of numerous mental problems that make modern personal problems a social and aggregated phenomenon. In this book, we discuss mental health problems on a micro level of a person's life and activity, and we use choice theory[2] as an interpretative tool for explaining the origin of mental crisis which explains reality psychotherapy.

By applying some processes that are characteristic of the late modern period, and the human biological development to choice theory constructs, our work answers the research question; how should a person actualize and conserve or regain his mental health

---

[2] Choice theory is a new kind of psychology that explains that we choose everything we do for different practical reasons – including the dissatisfaction we feel. We alone chose our activity and thoughts, and, indirectly, also our feelings and the best part of our physiology (Glasser 1998).

considering his biological basis, concepts and perceptions of modernity, and the consequent psychic crises. With the defined research question we want to redirect the research focus from the question "what is a person" to the neglected question "who is a person" and to his living and social dimension. The claim that a person has the power to influence the consciousness, the recognisability, the tangible, the presence here and now, will be the most important directive of the projected work in which the person will be treated as a subject, a social agent on a relation level and in a corresponding social framework.

The emphasis of the monograph is on the definition of a person as a social, free, and responsible being who is intrinsically motivated and whose behaviour is purposive and proactive. This kind of thinking is in contrast with more notable and conventional approaches, which treat "mental illness" as an exclusively physiological biochemical dysfunction within a person, for which neuropharmacology and a growing consumption of medicaments have an important role in eliminating unwanted feelings and behaviours. With this kind of understanding we avoid dealing with the basic factors of augmenting mental distresses and we overlook the role of the most important agent in a social activity – a person whose behaviour is reflected on the face of modern society.

The centre of this work is the modern evolution-systematic approach to the discussion of mental health problems, so-called choice theory – reality psychotherapy, which gives an interdisciplinary interpretation and understanding of psychic crises in contrast with the existing traditional approaches.

Regarding a medical model of mental illness and the role of the "mental patient", there are numerous discussions taking place within sociological and humanistic sciences. Those discussions are triggering determined epistemological shifts in science that are also perceived by the so-called praxeological sciences. In this work, we will try to thematize them by studying the subject in a broader socio-cultural context and to show the meaning of the integral approach in treating mental health problems.

The research is based on the anthropology of health, illness, and treatment, which introduces us to a way in which people understand the world, to the characteristics of human social systems and values, to the understanding of everyday satisfactions, and the manifestations of pain. Based on historic and systematic analysis of illnesses and clinical practices, a basic paradigmatic framework of health anthropology was developed. It is based on the presumption that health and illness are cultural constructs and that their manifestations are part of a determined society's cultural patterns. Culturally determined concepts of normality and abnormality are formed within a specific social space and form the theory of illness and health. Regardless of the manners of manifesting dissatisfaction and sufferance in various cultures around the world, the manifestation of human distress has become a universal human phenomenon. In this context, along with a constant augmentation of mental problems, we emphasize socially more acceptable ways of expressing emotional dissatisfaction according to social gender.

In accordance with our chosen theory, we assume that an ineffective satisfaction of psychical needs and the use of external control psychology behaviours in a modern person's everyday reality can manifest itself in various destructive ways regarding the creativity of an individual's system. That is why we conclude the research work by analysing erroneous beliefs of external control psychology and, mostly in the empiric part of the monograph, we confront the consequences of its use for interpersonal relationships and an individual's mental health.

The empirical part of the monograph is based on the scientific approach of quality research, specifically on the case study of psychotherapeutic practice. The plural study makes it possible to identify the repeating of determined characteristics and reinforces the representation of intended patterns. The case study demonstrates a psychotherapeutic process of clients with manifestations of various psychic crises, who were included in psychotherapeutic treatment held by me. We studied the client's dissatisfaction with his present reality – an incompatibility of the quality world with the material word and the variety of creative behaviours in frustrating situations. We will learn about the motivation system, based on the internal origin of human behaviour, and by understanding the integral behaviour I will present the interactions between body (somo) and mentality (psyche). The transcription of the therapeutic dialogue is an attempt to thoroughly present the use of external control psychology behaviours in the client's life and important relationships. The therapeutic process is orientated towards the client's replacement of destructive behaviours of external control psychology with a more effective choice theory, which enables him to regain control over his life. Besides the importance of relationships, we emphasize and explicitly present the meaning of the relationship between the therapist and the client in the sense of a therapeutic means for reaching a goal.

An important part of the message that this work tries to convey is that the absence of illnesses does not yet imply mental health. It is necessary to change the conviction that a person is (biophysically, mentally, and socially) completely determined and to search for possibilities which develop mental (not just physical) health. That is why studying reality therapy within the context of anthropological-sociological perspectives is contemporary and scientifically relevant for two reasons: to substantiate the theoretical framework of studying the origin of mental health problems and as an applicative research study with the final ambition to define guidelines for changing the perception of a modern person's mental health.

With this kind of writing we are not rejecting science; on the contrary, we are stepping on the side of real science with an interdisciplinary approach to treating mental health problems because "real science in its search for understanding and progress does not exclude any possibility" (Lynch in Glasser 2003, 13). With the transition from the concept of a mental problem to a model of health, our work represents a real image of new possibilities for understanding a person's mental health. The subjects treated in this book are placed in the existing modern movements and trends in the sphere of psychotherapy that stand up for the deinstitutionalization of psychiatric services, for the treatment of mental health problems outside psychiatric practice, and for the normalization of the life of people with mental health problems and their self-actualization.

The book *Mental Health in Modern Society* brings into question the basic psychology and explains, based on theoretical concepts and psychotherapeutic practice, the possibility that another type of psychology may exist, the psychology of personal freedom.

THE SOCIOLOGICAL-ANTHROPOLOGICAL CONTEXT OF THE LATE MODERN SOCIETY

Theoreticians define the condition of late modern society[3] based on tensions among various ambivalences: individuality and plurality, locality and globality, production and reproduction, virtual and actual reality, reality and hyper-reality, and a subject positioned as a centre and one removed from the centre position. The new conditions in the social reality of late modernism are reflected in new interpersonal relationships, new fears and risks, tension between local and global, and new relationships within the consumerist culture. We define the late modern period as a period of pluralized society and new forms of social relationships, a period of a fragmented and individualized person, a period of globalized consumerism, many choices, and new risks (Bauman 2002, 2007; Beck 2001, 2003; Giddens 1991, 2000).

According to Beck, the late modern society is a high-risk society, which introduces new forms of risks and danger and it is built on the reflection of the previous situation (Beck 2001, 11–19). Modern institutions are becoming globalized and daily life distances itself from traditions and usages that were always present in previous periods. Late modernism affects absolutely all spheres of social life, and carries risks particularly on the level of individual and interpersonal relationships.

Giddens (1991) perceives the changes of the radicalized or reflexive modernism as well; however, his concept of late modernism assumes a greater continuity with modernism than Beck's concept of risk society. Giddens' general assumption is that it is possible

---

[3] The English sociologist Anthony Giddens (1991) and some other critics and theoreticians name the modern social condition, the condition of the 21th century, a high or late modernism and not postmodernism. They believe that the prefix post is misleading because (in a linguistic sense) it indicates something that comes after, that substitutes the previous condition. The use of the concept of late modernism was justified as being more of a progress of the characteristics of modernism and not its replacement. Despite acknowledging some characteristics of postmodernism, Giddens believes that we have not yet reached it and that modernism is still developing.

to consciously manage modern societies to a certain extent, while Beck accents the unintentional side effects as the driving force of progress.

Giddens' study of modernization places Beck's thesis in a socio-psychological and sociological context. On the subject of living in a "risk society", Giddens believes that it is merely a calculative approach to whether the positive or negative opens the possibilities, choices, and acts with which we are constantly confronted as individuals or groups in modern social situations (ibid. 15). According to Giddens' (2001) structuration theory, the society and the individual have a two-way effect. An individual's actions and their way of developing create a structure, which in turn effects the individual and enables him to function. So, the individual with his actions affects and changes the society, and in the meantime also changes himself in accordance with the reactions of society. All big changes that take place in a society and bring new, unknown or less expressed risks, demand a new evaluation of social life.

The analysis of the cultural situation in late modernism shows the increase of identity incertitude, disorientation, loss of the centre and depth, and the emphasizing of short duration, fluidity, and variability (Bahovec 2005, 140). Unlike the constant investment in the technological and economic progress of Western society, the culture of social relationships remains unchanged. Furthermore, with society's remarkable scientific and economic progress we still witness numerous destructive phenomena[4], which present the individual as more and more vulnerable on a personal, relational, and social status level.

Individualization and Formation of Relationships in Late Modern Society

The challenges of modern society come mostly from individualization[5] and pluralism, which means a multitude of possible choices and decisions that an individual has to face nowadays. Beck believes that by creating social networks and also being active in other fields, one becomes a being of choices,[6] "a being of possibilities"—*homo options* (Beck

---

[4] The typical destructive phenomena of modernism and late modernism are: occurrence and increase of various chemical and nonchemical types of addiction, increase of mental health problems, increase of violent behaviour, including suicides and murders, relationship and family problems. I quote the relationship problems as a part of post modernistic symptomatology, and at the same time I present relationships as the cause of the phenomena, discussed as destructive for the individual and society.

[5] Beck (2001) uses the concept of individualization for naming the processes of prestructuring and dynamization of lifestyles in Western society. He understands individualization as "eradicating"/ "liberating" (*disembedding*) from the original frame of an everyday life and daily social relationships (ibid). The individualization represents social processes characterized by the melting of life forms that are regulated and standardized in advance, for example class affiliation, gender roles, nuclear family, etc., and by disintegration of organized biographies and life orientations (Ule and Kuhar 2003, 22).

[6] Sande defines the choice of a modern man as a choice between life, death, physicality, identity, religion, marriage, parenting, mobile phones, drugs, etc. (Sande 2004, 12).

1998). The selectiveness brings an individual to make decisions followed by risks[7] that he cannot anticipate and control entirely. That is why individualization of an individual means more conflicts, breaks, and risks. He cannot be sure whether he has made a right decision, but at the same time the democratization of a person's individualization enables more choices and freedom (Beck and Beck-Gernsheim 2006, 90; Beck 2002).

The partiality of society offers an individual a multitude of choices, numerous roles, and at the same time the loss of a unified social frame. In opposition to the predictable answers of a traditional social environment, the future of late modernism enables numerous different alternatives, among which an individual chooses himself (Giddens 1991, 73). Therefore, his choice is a constant search for balance between possibility and risk (ibid).

According to Beck, the process of individualization in the flexible postmodern society, or in the society of "second modernism"[8], appears more and more as the individual's "liberation" from the forces of everyday life's leading social frames—as the loss of traditional pillars and the increase and individualization of social risks and inequality connected to it; as the submission and addiction to social institutions, etc. (Beck 1992).

Primary individualization concerns three dimensions: the dimension of liberating individuals from historically predefined social forms, from traditional relationships of domination and supplying; the dimension of growing up, which means the loss of traditional certainty and transparency, how to do something, the loss of trust in the leading social norms; and the dimension of control or reintegration and of relationships among people, who form them according to their personal interests, will, and especially lifestyles (ibid).

Bauman understands the issue of individualization as "transformation of 'identity' from 'endowment' to 'task' and as assigning the agents the responsibility of performing these tasks and the consequences (also side effects) of their operations" (Bauman 2002, 42). But he also points out that now and once—on the fluent[9] and simple, and the solid and difficult level of modernism – individualization is a destiny, not a choice. It is not possible to avoid individualization and refuse to collaborate in the game of individualization. The

---

[7] The systematic theoretician Niklas Luhmann distinguishes between the concepts of risk and danger, wherein "with distinguishing he supposes that there is an uncertainty linked to the future damage. We can explain the possible damage as a consequence of decision-making, so we attribute the damage to it. In this case, we talk about risk, namely about the risk of decision-making. We can explain the possible damage as something caused by external factors and so we attribute it to the environment. In this case, we talk about danger" (Luhmann 1997, 22).
[8] "Second modernism" is a term introduced into social theory by Beck (1994) to replace the concept of postmodernism. According to Beck, classic modernism is only part modern because it did not carry out the modernization processes.
[9] Bauman uses the concept of "fluid modernism" as a metaphor for the present level of the modern period. According to Bauman, the present is changing, that is why it retains it form with difficulty.

subject's freedom and the responsibility for the construction of its own identity structure have their price—the loss of the feeling of safety (ibid, 45).

Giddens (1990, 1991) also stresses the importance of individualization, which he perceives as the construction of identity through a coherent narration of a person's life as one of the bases of modern society. According to Giddens, there is no identity in the behaviour or in the reactions of other people: "Identity is not a distinguishing characteristic nor a collection of characteristics owned by an individual. It's oneself, reflexively comprehended by a person in the terms of his or her biography" (Giddens 1991, 53).

An optional or fiddled, reflexive or do-it-yourself biography, at the same time always a risky biography (Beck 1992) dictates decisions and choices that have responsibility as a consequence. An individual's understanding of the sense of his own actions enables him to see that he is responsible for his actions. "And that is the essence of personal identity: a subjective control over the actions for which we take an objective responsibility" (Berger in Luckmann 1999, 19).

According to Beck, individualization is an institutionalized individualism, which means that the basic human rights and responsibilities redirect more and more from groups and localities to individuals. That represents a complete turn in the ways of life, thinking, an individual's identity, and subjective structures; their interpersonal relationships; and social relations. This results in a turn from domination of class, gender, and cultural identities defined beforehand to an increasingly plural, individually determined, temporary, and relationally oriented lifestyle (Ule 2000, 51–52).

Individualization reduces the length and strength of interpersonal connections, strong communities, and the individual's obligation to those connections and communities (Dahrendorf in Ule 1994, 23). Therefore, it is not only the biography that is at risk but also an individual's social decisions. Thus, giving meaning to life depends on an individual's decisions, and therefore he cannot be considered as a victim of individualization, as part of a collective destiny, but as the creator of his own destiny. Individualization implies the subject's tendency to take destiny in his own hands.

Encouraging an individual to pursue only his own interests and satisfactions, and the interests and satisfactions of others only to the extent that they concern his own, causes shallowness and fragility in interpersonal relationships. There is no reciprocity or solidarity; there is only the prospect of an individual to acquire it, for it is an urgent psychological need, but the individual would not give it. The influence of individualization on interpersonal relationships results in the loss of continuity, durability, confidentiality, dedication, and reliability in interpersonal relationships. The modern individual creates fragile and hollow interpersonal relationships, which are without the basic sense of security and belonging and thus, cannot give him or her the possibility to establish a strong identity.

The occurrence of unconnected and disjointed relationships in society, oversaturation, and weakening of social ties leads to the emergence of an uncentred subject, who no longer has solid identity foundations (Gergen 1991). Being a subject of late modernity means to constantly be the subject of self-reflection, self-control, and to have an identity, which is a difficult project to achieve. The modern individual no longer lives a solid, continuous, and stable story. His "patchwork self-image"[10] can be composed of completely unconnected, separate, and temporary life stories. The possibility of an independent and the necessity of a constant choice-making, and moreover the creating of one's own identity, which the individual cannot shape into a logical image, manifest themselves in a form of deviation in the individual's life.[11]

The Identity Concept of a Late Modern Individuum Ad a Reflexive Subject[12]

An individual's self-awareness and perception—reflection of others—create late modern identities. The identity in the modern society reconstructs and redefines itself. The disappearing of the personal-centred oneself leads to a constant search of one's own identity and the formation of partial identities that compared to traditional identities are more variable, transitional, and less overloaded.

The individual of late modernism has the possibility to form identity, defined as a social construct, which originates in the society and is sustained by it, and also changes according to it. The self becomes the centre of actions in late modernism. The society becomes the instrument which enables the individual to form his or her individual life (Beck in Beck-Gernsheim 2006, 50). "Individualization in this sense means that the biography of people liberates itself from anticipated fixations, becomes open, dependent on decisions and it is laid in the hands of each individual as a duty" (Beck 2001, 197). So the self becomes a reflexive project, whose priority is self-actualization, the realization of the assumption of existential philosophy (who am I, what am I, and where I'm going).

---

[10] The modern type of identity is defined by terms such as "*patchwork identity*", "*jungle of the self*" (Beck) and "*bricolage identity*" (Lash).

[11] The inability to create logical identity is manifested as embitterment, depression, anxiety, addiction, eating disorders, hatred towards oneself or the world, violence against oneself or others; the final form of ripping one's self-image is suicide (Kobal Grum 2003, 183–184).

[12] The concept of reflexivity is interpreted differently by different authors. It could be as awareness, self-reference, and personal autonomy. Its use also varies according to different authors. This is why Beck (1994) requests the separation of two concepts: reflection (awareness) and reflexivity (unconscious self-reference). In this work, the concept is used in the sense of awareness.

Beck believes that social agents have to decide about their privacy, therefore to reflexively form their biographies. In his opinion, elective biographies are a reflection of an individual's autonomic action and "a response to the social situations outside privacy" (Beck v Giddens 2000, 213).

With the thesis that "the changes in the private aspects of a personal life are directly linked to larger social situations or that the reflexivity of modernity expands also to the essence of self" (Giddens 2000, 209), Giddens introduces the concept of the reflexive self-project. It consists of "coherent, but always revised biographic stories, it takes place in a context of various choices, which filtrates through abstract systems" (ibid). Identities were supplanted by unified sovereign selves. So, according to Weeks, identity has become a process and not something given, which "offers us the choice of staying, existing before the truth about us" (Weeks 1995, 31).

The meaning and influence of self-evidence that dictated the course of the individual's choice get lost, and so the prescribed life forms. A person creates his own biography according to his desires and ambitions, in which case he exposes himself to risks, but he is free, creative and could be completely innovative.

The self of a late modern subject is more autonomous, fluid, plural, and open to changes. In late modernism, the self becomes a reflexive project and the individual's identity a reflexive (conscious) project of a self that leads a person to the original core of a personal and social truth (Giddens 1991, 53). The individual identity is not determined and interpreted through tradition anymore, which is why Giddens (1991 33) believes that it is necessary to include self-reflexivity of the personality and life situations into individualization.

We have to understand the subject's self-realization as a "balance between a possibility and a risk" (Giddens 1991, 73). The change in the perception of risk in modern society changed with the loss of the known, the essential. On a theoretical level it is possible to connect the loss of balance and the basic confidence in our own abilities and the rightness of our choices to the concept of identity crisis and the loss of ontological security (ibid, 39) that the late modern theoreticians install into the discussion about complex situations of late modern societies. A person's life liberates itself from external control and constraints; it loses its external support, the sense of security, and its deepest identity (Beck and Beck-Gernsheim in Beck, Beck - Gernsheim, 2006, 57). The concepts and perceptions of modernism are subdued to doubts and scepticism; they are not comprehended anymore as something natural and non-questionable, but as constructs created by an individual alone (Bernardes 1997, 39). When Giddens talks about the aspiration to *clear relationships*, basically dependent on contentment and repayments that belong with these relationships and not on external contentment and repayments, he believes that the relationships become an elementary necessity, in the socio-psychological sense of clear relationships and relations, for the reflexive self-project (Giddens 2000).

Therefore, it is firstly necessary to place the construction of identity and social reality in the context of two levels: the self and inter-subjective exchanges.

Intersubjectivity of the Real-World Construction

The theory of symbolic interactionism, regarding the cognitive representation of the social world in a person, corresponds to the concept of "generalized other". According to Mead, the "generalized others", which enable a person's self-perception in a social environment, are values, ethical rules characteristic for a culture where a child socializes (Mead 1997, 103–167).

An individual is born into an objective social structure, where he or she is faced with important others that are responsible for his or her socialization. These important others are imposed on the individual. Their definitions of a person's situation are presented to him or her as an objective reality. He is not born only into an objective social structure, but into an objective social world. The important others, who pass this world to him, change it during the mediation. They choose the images according to their own position in the social structure and based on their own life-rooted characteristics (Berger and Luckmann 1988, 123–124).

Mead (1934) believes that not all the people that are part of an individual's various forms of relationships are equally important for the construction of one's self-image, but only some of them, the "important others". Those people have a special place in an individual's life and are part of his quality world.

The important others are definitely the parents who define the world the child has to internalize. According to Berger and Luckmann (1988), they modify it twice – as members of a culture and through their own life history. Parents co-shape the child's objective reality with their opinions. The child does not doubt what his important person says; he accepts their opinion as truth and in time, he makes it his own (Friebe 1993, 42–44).

The process of self-respect and self-valuation is connected to the opinion of "important others". Numerous authors (Snygg and Combs 1949; Rogers 1951, etc.) stress the need for a positive self-valuation as a basic human need.

Rogers (1951) asserts that a positive conception of personality or confidence in oneself and others is based on the parents' unconditional acceptance of their child and that a negative conception of oneself is based on the terms of strictness. Selective praise creates what Rogers calls conditions of worth; it makes the children believe that their parents' love depends on the possession of determined qualities and on certain behaviour. Instead of selective praise, in Roger's opinion, we should more effectively develop a child's positive self-esteem with unconditional acceptance, which means to respect and love the child without valuating his specific qualities.

Merkle (1996) believes that an individual's negative thinking about himself is inured. The internal critic, as he names it, evolves within the early years of a person's life. A child learns to look at himself through his parents' eyes and to talk to himself as they used to do. Everyone has an observer inside him who controls his behaviour and gives the final judgment. By pointing out his mistakes and weaknesses he attacks his self-confidence. The internal critic takes advantage of any chance, even an insignificant one, to humiliate the person and does not allow even the slightest possibility to make him feel better (Friebe 1993, 41). The internal critic is an "important other" who had an important influence on the child. The critic took over the values, ethical rules, and the life philosophy, everything the "important others" told him or her (Merkle 1996, 40–44).

It is necessary to understand the relation between a person and a social context regarding the socio-psychological interpretation of an individual's behaviour and his actions within the frame of two contradictory approaches: the "bottom-up" approach and the "top-down" approach (Burr 1995, 97). The first approach presumes that a person is a being concluded in himself, within whom private psychological processes evolve that fundamentally influence his reactions. The area of the society represents only an area of various dependent and independent variables that need to be controlled or excluded. But this approach disregards the contradictoriness and the partiality of a person's mental structure and the constant construction of the social world (Ule 2005, 27–28). The systematic view of a person and society comprehends the person as socially constructed through the totality of his social relationships, which is why the study of the consequences of social effects on individuals and the use of the upside-down approach are necessary. Ule stresses that the social construction is a process which can be as subjective as objective, individual, and social. It is a collective context and the source of human actions, its subjective and objective viewpoints (ibid, 28). The systematic conception of the relationship between a person and society and the concept of the social construction of reality besides the social interaction on all four levels of social activity – intrapersonal, interpersonal, group, and institutional-social – also includes the levels of the socio-psychological analysis and the explanations.[13] For studying the discussed theme, the individual and interpersonal level are especially relevant. Therefore, I emphasize the psychological subject and his psychological responses

---

[13] These levels were defined and analysed by Doise (1986). Beside the individual, interpersonal, and situational level, the social interaction also takes place on an institutional/positional and systematic/ideological level.

to social influences and psychological mechanisms that are important for his integration in a social interaction.

As the experimental studies show (Coopersmith 1967; Gergen 1977; Meyer 1983) the indirect feedback given by important people through their behaviour and a general relationship towards the individual, can have a big influence on his self-evaluation (Skalar 1990, 16). The basic model "The reflected appraisal process" (TRAP) (or, according to Cooley and Mead, "the mirror self") is composed of three elements: self-evaluation; the actual evaluation of "important others"; and the individual's perceptions of the evaluation of "important others". The theory poses two basic suppositions: that the evaluation of important others influences the reflective evaluation (subjectively interpreted feedback) and that the reflected evaluation influences the self-evaluation. The first postulate asserts that, to a certain extent, people sense correctly what others think about them. The second postulate suggests that an individual internalizes these reflective evaluations whether they are correct or not. The third postulate originates from the first two and states that the evaluation of "important others" directly influences one's self-evaluation; the effect would be noticeable if the reflective evaluations (the reflection of others' opinions) were not taken into consideration (Felson 1993). The studies show that there is a correlation among self-evaluation, the evaluation of "important others", and an individual's perception of the evaluations of "important others".

Schulz (2001, 138–139) warns us about the consequences of defined experiences that influence the formation of the concept of one's own self. The message of the relationship seems completely personal and could have a considerable long-term effect (ibid). In the process of primary socialization, from the viewpoint of a close social environment, the stereotypes, decisive for an individual regarding his looks and holistic behaviour, which influence the formation of an individual's role and posture, strengthen.

Mead (1997) defines an individual's social self as the segment of personality in which the subject absorbs and internalizes all the social contents he acquired during the socialization processes. However, the subject does not accept these contents passively, but at least from a defined period on, he processes them actively, selecting through a personal, operative self the segment of personality which is the operator of self-awareness and his own activity. Accordingly, Mead separates two stages of socialization: play and game. The first stage, the play, is the one before the appearance of the personal self; the second stage, the game, is the one after. This is a period where the subject already thinks about his behaviour and is autonomous in a sense or at least partly autonomous in taking his decisions, including the choice of the survival strategy.

Goffman (1959) warns us about the individual's "role playing" and "mask wearing" which are the representation of an individual's self-perception. But Buss and Briggs (1984) assert that social behaviour is frequently the consequence of a compromise between external expectations for keeping the appearance (self-presentation) and a person's individuality (Shaw 1997, 303).

Sullivan's interpersonal theory also discusses the meaning of the interaction with others for the development of self-image (Sullivan 1953). In his own way, Sullivan defines the role of "other people" in the development of one's self conception. He attributes the biggest importance to warm interpersonal relationships with important people that give to the individual a sense of security and protection (Ule 2000, 126). Sullivan defends the theory that all personal growth, and all the regress of personality, therapy, and the growth of personality originate from our relationships with others.

An individual's personal experience includes the so-called proprioceptive self,[14] which does not exclude the individual from forming his own image. Acquiring messages from others can never be merely a passive expression, a passive reflection of unfamiliar ideas, and opinions of other people. Our vision of other people's ideas is necessary and just ours. Through the proprioceptive data, we obtain an image of ourselves that others generally cannot pass to us and that is why this data is a deep psychological basis of our self and our self-image. Everything shows that the mirror, social data about us, somehow clings to this basic proprioceptive self-image (Musek 1992, 68).

The understanding of the relationship between society and personality represents a peculiar coexistence, co-dependence, for a person co-lives with others and among others. It is in human nature to construct a mental reconstruction of what one believes is real. One's findings depend on the experiences acquired during one's life, on the desires, needs and intentions one has towards others and oneself, for the social environment gains importance through the process of social activity (ibid, 99).

We build our own reality construction based on the received, formed, and processed data from the external world. We live in a sort of a "subjectively created and formed world" where we accept others and ourselves, where the external world has "certain characteristics only in relation with a social community of individual organisms that are in a reciprocal interaction" (ibid).

---

[14] The studies about social identity prove that people experience their world and define themselves according to their socio-cultural contexts (Asch, 1952; Gurin and Markus, 1988; Tajfel and Turner, 1985). Among the socio-cultural factors that influence the formation of a self-image, Oyserman and Markus add the historical, economic, and national-regional context; nationality, gender role, creed, and social status; family, friends, and important others; socially saturated self-image (Oyserman and Markus, 1993: 194).

Norbert Elias[15] (2000, 2001) reveals vaguely self-evident behavioural patterns of an individual's behaviour in society. In his opinion, the transformation in an individual's behaviour and long-term social changes occurred through the adjusting of individual outbursts of strong emotions with external constraint and self-constraint of changing the human behaviour and experience, and also partially through the changing of the structure of all human behaviours as such. In Elias's work, the possibility of a behavioural change presents itself as a *habitus* of self-control. In his work *About the Civilization Process* he talks about the evolutionary process that men experienced and about the historical changing of the relation between self-constraint and social constraint, when "the self-control apparatus strengthens up against the social constraint and civilization takes over the function of self-control habitus" (Elias 2001, 432). Elias introduces the concept of *homo clausus* as the perception of an individual, who is a small world to himself and exists as completely independently from the vast world outside himself (Elias 2000, 42).

According to Berger and Luckmann in the context of conceptualization of intersubjectivity, the reality of everyday life shows itself as an intersubjective world that the individual constantly shares with others through interaction and communication (Berger and Luckmann 1988, 30). This way, a relationship makes it to the forefront of a person's experience, because the experience gains a meaning only while in a relationship.

The basic question is how to remain a social subject, to acquire and maintain autonomy against the influences of social structure and other phenomena. On the one hand, we have an internal conflict within the subject, a rift between the preserving of one's self, one's personality, one's identity, and on the other hand, the principles of society and the opinions of "important others". Here we can see the conflict between the desired self-image, "as we want to be" and the normal self-image, "as we should be." With the disintegration of traditional forms, the modern psychological subject represents a plural and diverse system of self-images, his internal contrast is represented by the discrepancy between the desired and real self-image, which manifests through various destructive forms of behaviour. [16]

---

[15] Norbert Elias' approach includes various theoretical fields of sociology that are the result of the influence of sociologists such as Auguste Comte, Karl Mannheim, Karl Marx, Georg Simmel, and Max Weber. Elias' figurative sociology concentrates on the social processes and researches reciprocal connections or figurations among biology, psychology, sociology, and history of the evolutionary process that gave human beings the "ability to learn" (Dunning 1999,13).

[16] Lamovec has identified the primal cause for mental distress in an environment full of pressure and incomprehension, because the individual internalizes the environmental pressures and, in doing so, he experiences frustrations that turn into a sort of violence. She believes that suicides (as an extreme form), like other mental health problems, are just a symptom of violence that exists in society and does not originate from the individual, but from his confrontation with the world (Lamovec 1999, 77).

The Loss of Ontological Safety and the Crisis of Sense

The late modern disunity of living shows the uncertainty of anyone who enters the world of unpredictable situations, ontological emptiness, and lack of firm principles through inflexible patterns and routines. The question of safety has become a permanent concern of late modernism. It represents the loss of ontological security,[17] especially in the fact that the social world or the meaning of life is no longer objectively given, but the individual has to create his own personal meaning. The so-called un-centred subject becomes central, without a crucial or assigned position that can fit into a social context. Identity crises are frequent where the liberation of personal biography from the objective existential plan has occurred.

Giddens (1992) believes that ontological safety concerns the basic trust developed by an individual in his relationship with the world and himself. It is connected to the phenomenological to-be-in-the-world and it is mainly an emotional and not a cognitive phenomenon. In Giddens' opinion, confidence is not connected primarily to risk, but to the feeling of biographical continuity, which is an important part of ontological safety and the cornerstone of the feeling of a stable identity.

The new social condition requires from the individual active life choices and other daily activities. Individualization enables alternative life courses, as well as demands the individual's active engagement in formatting his personal biography (Beck and Beck - Gernsheim, 1996, 817).

Along with individualization and pluralization appears the co-called TINA syndrome – "there-is-no-alternative" – that orients the individual's activity inwards, towards himself. Because of the numb relationships between the individual and the structure, it focuses on the individual. The Becks describe today's society as a "highly individual society: create your own purpose" (ibid, 834). The bonds between the structure and the individual become paralytic and the individual's choices more and more autonomous.

Berger and Luckmann denote modern pluralism as the crucial factor that gives origin to purpose crises in society and in an individual's life. According to them, the consequences of modern pluralism show themselves in the relativizing of value systems and explanations that leads to the disorientation of an individual and of whole groups. "Anomie" and "alienation" are two categories that indicate the distress of a person who has to cope with the modern world (Berger and Luckmann 1999, 37). The authors conclude that in circumstances of individualism and pluralism, it is hard for individuals to find the

---

[17] Giddens (2000) introduces the concept of ontological safety, i.e. the trust that most people have in the continuity of personal identity and in the firmness of the social and material environment activity. The sense that we can count on people and things has a crucial importance in the narration of trust and it is based on the feeling of ontological security, swayed in the face of the risk society.

self-evident life orientation. They believe that modern pluralism leads to a great relativizing of the values system and "undermines this self-evident behaviour. The world, society, life, and identity are becoming more and more questionable." (ibid, 39)

Fromm explains how negative influences of liberalism and individualism, based on human needs, reflects on a personal self. He specifies which needs are existential and which needs are artificially created, and thus form the so-called individual's market character (Fromm 2004, 133–134). Fromm tackles social relationship critics related to today's capitalist-consumerist society, through the analysis of a pair of concepts: to have and to be. He sees these two concepts as diametrically opposite ways of life, as two different orientations of human behaviour and society. While searching for real reasons for the orientation towards acquisition and possession, Fromm ponders the orientation towards the essence of being, as the pylon of a new and more satisfying society. However, in its orientation towards the essence of being it is not about a new life dimension that man has yet to discover, but it is about a person's genuine nature that he has once lived, but lost (Babič 2005, 81). Here it is possible to identify the core of the Fromm's entire philosophy, which is based on the concept of separation: the person is separated from nature, his own true essence, fellow people, and his creativity (ibid).

In the concept of separation lies the source of human discontent; Fromm found the causes for people's various behaviours in a person's tragic disunity, oriented towards having. The humanism of Fromm's philosophy orientates the individual towards the essence of being, that "can appear as long as we lower the orientation towards having, which is not being – that is, when we cease searching for security and identity, as to cling to that what we possess, on our self and our belongings." (Fromm 2004, 83–84)

The human structure requires a created, constructed model of the world that can help a person interpret the events within the world. Our subjectively reshaped world is based on cognitive processes, on receiving and processing data that we acquire from the environment and represent the basis of the world we live in.

A person's individual world is created. This world is just a "perception of something" and it "exists only if he focuses his attention towards the object or the objective" (Berger and Luckmann 1999, 12). "The purpose is formed in the human consciousness; in a person's consciousness, which individualized itself in a certain body and grew into a person through social processes" (ibid). With the phenomenological definition of consciousness, the authors place the person as the creator of his own world and as the co-creator of social reality that realizes the imposed objective with his actions. They define the characteristics of the social construction of reality as the product of human activity and reciprocal relationships with the intertwining of the individual and social world.

MENTAL HEALTH – A SOCIAL AND PSYCHOLOGICAL PHENOMENON

With the process of deinstitutionalization, in recent decades mental health moved from the total institution of the psychiatric hospital to the community. The fall of total institutions enabled the anti-psychiatric movement to prepare an early social evaluation of mental distress. "Mental illnesses" [18] are not so remote and scary anymore, but they are present in all social structures.

The paradigm of anthropology of health supposes that health and illness are cultural constructs and that their manifestations are part of the cultural patterns of a specific society, which establish the concepts of normality and abnormality, the concepts of illness and health of a specific culture.

Contemporary anxiety is connected to the feeling of uncertainty regarding the social situation and social roles and the incessant pressure to adapt and change identity, which lead to feelings of stagnation and emptiness, inexistence, and insignificance that go along with it (Stein, Vidich and Manning White 1962, 134). Fromm believes that the numerous emotional and mental states, indicated by psychiatrics as anxieties, are in fact states of loneliness or fear of loneliness in the individual's psychological isolation and alienation from oneself and other people. Personal sources of anxiety are confusion, psychological disorientation, and uncertainty regarding norms, values, ideologies, and the general sense of things (ibid, 131–132).

Glasser (2006) also thinks that social isolation and alienation from oneself and others are characteristics of the modern complex society. He believes that the common problem

---

[18] We understand mental health problems as an individual's ineffective attempt to gain control over his life. "Our creativity is in itself a normal, constant process, and when we realize it, it is not an illness. If we name it 'mental illness' we free the person of all the responsibilities for what he has done, we do him and society a bad favour." (Glasser 2007a 97) The use of medical terminology (illness, disorder) strengthens the stigmatization of difference and emphasizes the biological component of the arisen problems. Given the above-mentioned reasons we put the words mental health in quotation marks.

of people with a diagnosis of mental health problems is their unhappiness, especially the integration in unhappy relationships[19], and that the destruction of relationships is caused by external control psychology, describing behaviours that people use to change others (ibid).

A person's attempt to control another person's behaviour and to insist on his belief that it is possible to force someone to do what we want, is destructive for the whole society "if the system of values in the society stipulates that the community and the community of sense should overlap, therefore people have to live in communities, to coordinate their experiences and activities. In this case, a single incompatibility in the sense […] triggers a crisis of sense in the community […]" (Berger and Luckmann 1999, 21).

Different suppositions about the illness dictate the consideration of the social extension of a person's life and a larger model of health, i.e. the bio-psychological model, which is based on a biological, psychological, and social health conditioning (Kaplan, Sallis and Patterson 1993). The totality of the person's extensions includes his behaviour towards himself, others, his place in society, and is reflected through his integral activity. [20]

The condition for mental health is set by a mental coherence, as stated by the American-Israeli medical sociologist Aron Antonovsky[21] who developed the concept of salutogenesis along with the existing concept of pathogenesis. A person reaches an emotional, mental, and behaviouristic balance by developing a sense of harmony with himself – a coherence, a feeling of connection with others, involvement in relationships with others, a contribution and participation with loved ones, and a sense of understanding and accepting from others (Antonovsky in Kobolt and Rapuš Pavel 2009, 3).

Sapir explains that in his everyday activities an individual does not adapt to society, but to personal relationships (Sapir 1994, 204) which represent a link between the individual and society. The meaning of fulfilling relationships is not limited to family ties and friendships, but it stretches to a larger social environment, where individuals create the

---

[19] "When someone's relationships with people who means a lot to him are worse than he would like, then those kinds of relationships could be accompanied by various symptoms described in DSM-IV, a large collection of unhappy relationships, with broken marriage relationships in the forefront." (Glasser 2006, 15)

[20] The basic premises of a person's activity and his connection to a larger society represents the dimensions of mental health: suprapersonal, physiological, emotional, behavioural, cognitive, and the social political system (Groder in Tudor 1996, 25).

[21] Antonovsky (1991) studied people that survived extreme situations. He worked mostly with survivors of concentration camps. A defined group of people was physically and mentally unaffected by these happenings, while others become chronically ill, depressive, or had momentary suicidal thoughts. He discovered that among the members of both groups there are important differences in some mental characteristics – the sense of understanding (a person sees the world and life as understandable, structured, and ordered); the sense that things have a sense (a person believes in the sense of living), and the sense of control (a person trusts in his own capacities).

so-called social capital that enables them to have a successful actualization by creating connecting relationships.

Good relationships with others remain distant until a person realizes that the external control behaviour (changing, directing, forbidding, punishing, etc.) of another person is an impossible task. An individual's personal identity – his quality world – is created subjectively, that is why others cannot understand it or take it into consideration if he does not recognize it as individual and belonging to someone else. Tolerance is the highest value; it is the considering of someone else's quality world.

This is why the question regarding mental health is directly linked to the question of ethics. In explaining this question, Fromm starts from a person's basic psychic needs and the individual's holistic behaviour. "The respect for life, for others as well as for oneself, is a fellow passenger of life itself and it is a condition for mental health. [...] Even though a person does not care about destructive inclinations or he tries to defend them, he cannot, his body cannot restrain from responding to them and be hurt by actions that go against the principle, which supports his life and even all life [...]" (Fromm 2002, 168).

The awareness of individuality, the uniqueness of the human being, means the respect for diversity, "I also know that people have a perspective of the common world that is not identical to my own perspective. My 'here' is their 'there'. My 'now' does not equal their 'now' (Berger and Luckmann 1988, 30–31) and the need to create harmony, my 'plans' are different from the plans of others and they may even oppose them. In short, I realize that I live with others in a common world. The most important discovery is that there is a continuous connection between their meanings and mine and that I share with them the senses of the reality of the world." (ibid)

The Conceptualization of Mental Health

In contrast to the modern era, the late modern era is more inclined towards humanism and the ethical attitude,[22] which influences the differently conceptualized occurrence of the phenomenon of mental health. Mental health problems are not a medical phenomenon anymore – mental illnesses, linked to evil spirits in pre-modern societies, the later cramming of fools into madhouses, asylums, and total institutions, which enforced a stigmatized, patronising, and psychiatric view of the handicap.

---

[22] Beck (2001) labels the modern period as the period of totalitarian systems and systems that were based on the exclusion of specific population groups. Beck also talks about the period that constructed the concept of 'the other' (2001 7). It is possible to recognize the stereotypic perceptions of dominant ideologies in the forms of racism, sexism, anti-Semitism, colonialism, biologism, Freudism, etc.

The concept of mental health was transformed; it became also a social and psychological phenomenon. The integration of a psychological insight of a person's personality into medicine means defining mental health by dividing the personality in the individual's relation towards oneself, the realization of potentials, the independence from social influences, self-respect, feeling, the perceiving of the world, and the control of one's own life. Researching one's behaviour and performing social roles, meeting social expectations linked to defined roles, the quality of interpersonal relations, the relation towards the social environment, and defining normal and abnormal or deviant behaviour from the standard of specific roles, all that defines mental health as a social phenomenon (Freeman and Giovannoni 1969). The factors of mental health are determined by the factors of a psychological, biological, social, economic, or cultural source, which originate from a family structure, or from the quality of interpersonal relationships (ibid, 678).

The World Health Organization still considers the diagnosis as the key assumption of an illness,[23] while Levi Strauss formed the definition that "the health of an individual spirit includes taking part in a social life, as well as rejecting social life (however this rejection is possible only within the modalities imposed by the social life itself), corresponds to the occurring of mental disorders. The various forms of mental illnesses are distinctive for any society and the percentage of individuals affected by these disorders is constitutive for a special type of balance, specific for every independent society. So, for example, in societies that know shamanism, shamanistic behaviour is accepted as normal." (Levi Strauss and Mauss 1996, 237–238)

The classifications of behaviour as a mental illness within the medical discourse present the procedures of asserting morality over the body of treatment, which is based on a medical and exclusively organic conception of mental illness. The treatment techniques used by psychiatrists are applied on the body and not on the subject's spirituality. The purpose of those medicaments is to visibly calm down the "fools" in order to adapt their behaviour to normal norms (Kovačič 2008).

In the second half of the 20th century, the followers of antipsychiatry, Foucault (*Madness and Civilization* 1961), Szasz (*The Myth of Mental Illness* 1960) and Goffman (*Asylums* 1961), defined mental problems in a socio-functional way. Szasz (1982) understands the meaning of the mental illness phenomenon as a hidden fact, that most people's lives are an incessant struggle, not for the biological existence but for the sole peace of mind, or

---

[23] According to the *World Health Organization* 'the state of a mental illness' includes 'mental problems and burdens, weakened functions that are connected to distress, symptoms and mental disorders, that could be diagnosed, such as schizophrenia and depression.' *(World Health Organization, 2010)*

any other value or signification.[24] He claims that mental illness is a myth: "the concept of mental illness is used primarily to hide the fact that for most people, their lives are a struggle for survival, not in the sense of biological survival as much as in the sense of assuring one's 'place under the sun' " (Szasz 1960, 118). Szasz points out the powerlessness of hospitalized people as doctors don't take into account their opinion and devaluate their judgment.

Flaker also warns about the changing of reality in medical treatments. He believes that words invented by psychiatrists have two basic characteristics: they name and exclude, "naming a specific type of illness or any illness can transform a person into an object of psychiatric treatment, a chaotic situation in a settled one by excluding the scapegoat." (Flaker 1997, 3)

The concept of medical standards as defining norms and deviations from the norms and the medicine's task to return all the patients to a "normal" condition is defined by Foucault (1975). The normality techniques showed themselves as neutral and impartial. They enabled the categorization of deviant subjects with medical and psychiatric methods and they defended determined forms of disciplining the subjects, which leaned toward the removal of deviations. The illnesses became more important than the patients and medicine became the main institution of social control (Ule 2003, 237).

White (1988 20) believes that "insanity is a political-biological rebellion against the repressive normality, fear, and the concordance wherein people are afraid to think and behave differently." Rovatti offers a similar definition: "we can define insanity as difference and fear of difference. An insane person is a certain prototype of a different person: as in the past, when people shut an insane person in a special institution in order to confirm their own normality, so today the separation and ousting of different people continues, so a group can consolidate their own certain identity." (Rovatti 2004, 9)

Actually, "a mental illness is for now only an assumption in the cognitive-theoretical sense. We can neither prove it nor disprove it. The supposition of an illness harms the people marked with it. It leads to a life of stigmatization, which works as a self-realizing prophecy" (Lamovec and Flaker 1993, 88). This is like the Pygmalion effect (Rosenthal), when an individual behaves in accordance with the ideas and expectations of another person, without really having the problems attributed to him by others. The concept of stigma is established, defined by Goffman as a discrediting identity, where an 'abnormal'

---

[24] It is necessary to warn about the problem of dealing with and treating children with the drug Ritalin in attention deficit and hyperactivity disorder – ADHD. About the damaging effects of Ritalin and other stimulants, and about other possible non-medical forms of treatment in: Peter Breggin: Ritalin Fact Book (2002), Talking Back to Ritalin (2001), Reclaiming Our Children (2000), Medication Madness (2008), and Mary Ann Block: No More Ritalin: Treating ADHD Without Drugs (1996).

difference conceals all the other characteristics and marks them to the point of setting the owner of such an attribute in an inferior position in society. It is a relation that is dependent on the normative expectations of the environment (Goffman 1981).

The predominating biological model of modern psychiatry is openly criticized by the Irish psychiatrist Lynch, who believes that "the medical approach to mental distress is based on unproven suppositions, especially on the theory claiming that the basic cause of a mental distress is biological, an issue of biochemical imbalance, or genetic irregularity, or both. Psychiatry convinced itself and the public in general, that this is not a supposition, but a proven fact [...] After several decades and an intensive psychiatric research, they still cannot determine the biological cause for any psychiatric condition. The insufficiency of biological proofs confirms the uncommon fact that not one psychiatric diagnosis can be confirmed with a biochemical, radiological or any other laboratory test. I am not familiar with any other medical profession that would cure people based on a supposed biochemical irregularity." (Lynch v Glasser 2003, 6)

In accordance with Lynch's critics, Glasser (2003) understands mental health as something completely separate from 'mental illness' which he does not acknowledge, because he understands all 'psychopathological' behaviours'[25] as creativity of the brain through which a person wants to reduce frustration and satisfy his basic needs. By understanding the holistic behaviour of choice theory, he exchanges cause and consequence – the chemical imbalance in the brain is the consequence of chosen behaviours (to satisfy the needs) and of created beliefs (on the basis of the perceived system).

The theorists of positive conceptualization of mental health defend the need for the separation of mental health continuums and mental illnesses. Downie (in Tudor 1996, 24–25) explains the idea of separation of both concepts as a division that enables an individual to have a diagnosed mental illness, and at the same time to reach a high level of mental health and well-being. Seeing as the concepts of mental health and mental illness would belong to the same continuum, there would only be two options – an individual could be mentally healthy or mentally ill.

The distinction between mental health and mental illness, and the acknowledgement of mental health as a positive concept which is not defined by the absence of mental illnesses, are also defended by Tudor (1996), Adams, Amos, and Munro (2002). Tudor stresses that the line of separation between the two concepts is often erased. Mental health is still connected to the sphere of mental illness, which classifies both in the same continuum (Tudor 1996, 24).

---

[25] Glasser acknowledges the concept of mental illness only with a concrete pathology of the brain, such as epilepsy, Alzheimer's disease, genetic defect, for example Down syndrome, and similar. He also considers schizophrenia a holistic behaviour, not an illness (Lojk 2002).

Glasser (2003) defines mental health problems as an independent entity and not just the absence of an illness. The socio-emotional components of life, like a satisfying family life, friendly relationships, placement in a community, physical and mental health estimation, and their insufficiency express themselves through social deprivation (Andrews and Withey 1976; Bradburn and Caplovitz 1965; Inkeles 1998).

Glasser's definition of mental health [26] is radically constructed and it demolishes the concepts of normality and abnormality, established in society. The understanding of mental health is positioned in the context of good and satisfying relationships with close people, which enable a person to appease his psychical needs. The definition is conceived in such a manner that introduces an individual to the reflection of his own well-being and behaviour, and it directs them to a subjective experiencing and active functioning. At the same time, it warns us about the fact that mental health should be treated as an integral part of the sphere of public health.

The Manifestation of Mental Crises in Modern Society

The psychologizing of mental health is becoming a socially more acceptable form of manifesting emotional dissatisfaction in the modern, highly developed society. The expression of distress with mental pain runs parallel with the processes of individualization, which triggers disintegrative processes on the level of social relationships, culture, and an individual's identity. The self-definition of one's self is influenced by a strongly psychologized medical discourse, that helps the de-stigmatization of resolving psychic crises with the assistance of a professional and it also helps the augmentation of psychotherapeutic practices, since not so long ago, it was more acceptable and less discriminatory to somatise mental disorders.

It is estimated that 50 million people (11 per cent of the European population) suffer because of mental crises, which are diagnosed as mental disorders within the medical model. Depression is the most diffused medical problem in the EU, which according to the data from the member countries still remains socially and culturally more acceptable for women. According to the World Health Organization data, mental health problems are still increasing, and medical experts predict that in 2020 depression will be the most frequently diagnosed illness in the developed world (EUROPE, 2018).

---

[26] "You are mentally healthy and you enjoy the company of most of the people you know, especially important people from your life, like family and friends. In general, you like people and you are ready to help an unfortunate family member, a friend, or co-worker to feel better. You do not have major tensions in your life, you laugh a lot, and you rarely feel any of the pains that most people accept as an inevitable part of life. You enjoy life and you do not find it difficult to accept the fact that people are different. The last thing that could cross your mind is to criticize or try to change others. You use a lot of creativity in your activities and you probably use all your potentials, as you think possible. When problems arise, you feel sad – no one can always be happy – but you know why you are sad and you try to do something about it." (Glasser 2003, 37)

There are two culturally acceptable samples of emotional distress manifestation: drinking alcohol, and suicides and attempted suicides. Women are more prone to neuroses and depression. The manifestation of pain occurs within the defined gender roles and a defined cultural context. Therefore, those are manifestation forms of mental suffering, attributed to women or men, and with these forms they emphasize a typical woman's or man's behaviour (Podgornik 2012).

Alcoholism is considered to be the most frequent form of addiction in the Western world (Glasser 2000, 209), culturally and socially the most acceptable and tolerated form of destructive behaviour.

The research shows that the (ab)use of alcoholic drinks represents one of the key problems of public health. Numerous negative short-term and long-term medical and social results appear in peoples' medical conditions, their disease, and mortality rate. An excessive use of alcohol also has economic effects, due to a lower productivity, diseases, premature deaths, and expenses in medical care, traffic, and judicature (traffic accidents caused by drunk participants, temporary absence from work because of diseases, injuries, and poisoning, which are a direct consequence of alcohol consumption, etc.) (ibid).

Glasser's assessment is that "alcohol, opposite to other drugs, is an accepted and almost exalted part of our culture. Alcohol supports the cultural ideal – it helps us regain control over our life. The fact that alcohol is the most destructive force in our culture, making people lose their control, is not accepted and it will not be. [...] The culture, or at least the culture declared by the mass media, conducts it as a positive force, which it could be if consumed in normal quantities. [...] Alcohol is a type of drug that helps us do things, regaining control, which makes it a sign of strength and maturity if we can control it. It strengthens the sense of control and that is why we accept it instead of fearing it, which would be the correct thing to do." (Glasser 1994,131)

In the last forty-five years, the frequency of suicides in the world has augmented by approximately 60 per cent. Suicide is the leading cause of premature death in Europe – 58,000 cases per year, there are ten times as many suicide attempts (EUROPE, 2018).

The use of illegal drugs is increasing, wherein the age limit of users is lowering.

In the period from 1999 to 2005 in the EU, the percentage of people receiving medical treatment for the first time because of cocaine problems increased from 11 to 24 per cent of all new people who are receiving treatment. More than 12 million Europeans have used cocaine once in their lives; its use is most diffused among young adults. The drug is still in the domain of men (at a ratio of five men to one woman), but drug abuse is also becoming socially acceptable for girls.

The use of substances shows the purpose of choosing a destructive and ineffective behaviour, maybe even more than other painful behaviours – getting depressed,[27] suffering from a phobia, etc. Alcohol or any other drug[28] imitates or activates the chemical activity of the brain that induces a feeling of comfort. That gives a person the feeling that one or more of their needs are being satisfied and that they have control over their life (Glasser 2003). Getting drugged up is a dysfunctional form of solving problems. A drug can rapidly and without any effort relieve one's distress, solve the conflicts, and improve a bad condition, but the satisfaction lasts only as long as the effect of the drug. In order to regain a good feeling, one has to get drugged up again, which leads to addiction.

Besides getting drugged up with a substance, drugging with detrimental behaviours, the so-called nonchemical form of addiction,[29] which represents a modern way of manifesting dissatisfaction and a destructive attempt to gain control over one's own life that could be extremely risky and also potentially fatal for an individual.

The Humanistic-Existential Understanding of a Person

At the end of the fifties the mechanistic view of behaviourism and the biological reductionism and determinism of classic psychoanalysis (Friedman 1994) promoted the formation of a humanistic-orientated psychology or "third force", as Maslow named it.

Humanistic psychology tries to place the person as a holder of the phenomenological area of his own growth, contrary to the cognitive approaches, where the person is represented as a rational and predictable system.

The main points of humanistic psychology were also supported by Rogers in his theory. "In today's psychology, the fact that a subjective individual has an important value it is a

---

[27] In the present text, we have replaced the medical terminology and the terminology of external control psychology with the language of choice theory. The use of the gerund (depressing, being stubborn, having phobias, annoying, criticizing…) orients the client to an active view of his behaviour and to the possibility of choosing a more satisfying one, in spite of the medical model of illness that perceives the illness as a product of external factors, on which an individual has no effect (the patient fall sick with depression, he was affected by depression, he suffers from depression…)

[28] Drugs are substances that alter the sensory and emotional perception, consequently they offer a person a momentary and strong feeling of control (alcohol, cocaine) – the world is more beautiful, simple and pleasant (marihuana, LSD); a feeling of pure satisfaction can be offered by opiates, that operate directly on our control system (heroin, morphine, codeine); in order to calm the behaviour system (insomnia, anxiety) doctors prescribe barbiturates. The use of an intoxicating drug is a reflection of dissatisfaction and a desire for feeling better, for taking control over one's own life, which gets more and more out of control by taking drugs. When a drug gets to the brain, it enables a special rapture, a false feeling of control. But drugs have an even more detrimental influence on the actual loss of control over one's life, because drug abuse causes a psychical (pleasure) and physical (it becomes the chemistry of the body) addiction.

[29] It is a process of drugging with a form of behaviour, which has the characteristics of a psychoactive substance, changing the neurochemical activity of the brain (Carnes 2006).

rare standpoint, but an essential one. Regardless of how others characterize and valuate an individual, he is mainly and predominantly a human." (Rogers in Friedman 1994).

Phenomenology, a variant of the humanistic tradition, represents the basic cues of Rogers's theory. It supposes that the truth lies within the experience and not in objective descriptions of an individual's behaviour, the measurements and testing with natural sciences technics. Viewing a personality, Rogers takes a phenomenological standpoint, which expresses equality and the uniqueness of and individual.

He emphasizes that an individual perceives the world in his own unique way (Stražar 1975). He takes experience as the highest authority: "My own experience is the criterion for evaluating things. The idea (my own and of others) is not as important as my experience. I always have to return to the experience in order to find the truth forming inside of me. My own experience will not be influenced by the Bible, the prophets, Freud, researches, God's and man's revelation. My experience is not the greatest measure because it should be infallible, but because I can test it again and again in a new way. That way, its frequent errors are always open to correction." (Rogers 1995, 23–24). The essence of an individual is in his thoughts and feelings through his own personal experience.[30]

The assertion that the basis for explaining a personality is a person's subjectivity, his world of experiences and phenomena, is shared by some important psychologists. "Everything we perceive and think is part of our experiences – phenomena. The world we are part of is the world we see. Only the world as we see it and experience it has a meaning and a sense for us." (Lewin 1935; Snygg and Combs 1949 in Musek, 2003, 213).

Contrary to objectivistic psychology, psychological sciences use the subjective, the phenomenal world of an individual as a standpoint, according to which Rogers separates three types of realizations: the subjective realization, a realization within its own phenomenal area or realizations regarding their own referential framework; the objective realization, meaning that what we know is once again tested with others' observations; and the third, the interpersonal realization, which Rogers also calls a phenomenological realization and it represents the key to understanding someone else, basically to understand someone else's phenomenological area by using our sympathising capacities (Stražar 1975).

According to Ornstein (1973), a man has the capacity and attribute of limiting and transforming the stimuli he perceives, he is capable of "re-interpret", "reconstruct", "reprogram" (himself). A man interprets (again), (re)constructs – sets, tunes his perception based on past experiences, expectations and needs, aspirations, and intentions. He also uses this ability to expel regularities from the area of his perception. The phenomenon

---

[30] "The internal view" of a personality appeared through centuries in various forms, each having its own name – humanism, existentialism, phenomenology, and others.

is known as "habit" or "automatization" and it is enabled by the characteristics of a man's senses and his core nervous system to further select and build the stimuli input, so they can react to its changes. This is why a person's perception is a reciprocal interactive process between the environment (a stimuli reality, firstly selected with a biological structure and secondly with further interpretation mechanisms) and an individual's constantly corrected interpretations, constructions, descriptions, world models. Therefore, an individual selects the (sensory) input, he sets himself to an adequate (cerebral) output, he categorises and builds his perception based on his interpretations, his present and past experiences, his thoughts and emotional conditions, his aspirations, needs and expectations, his language, personal history of social interactions and social and cultural interpretations, and provisions (ibid).

Social interactions or experiences and an individual's behaviour in a social context are dependent on the standpoints.[31]

Ule believes that standpoints help to organise and structure an individual's view of the world. At the same time, they influence his perceptions, experiences of a determined situation, an object, they orient his attention, his perception, they influence his learning and remembering, they protect us (from everything that could hurt us), and help us build our self-image. We use them to express our values and they help us adapt and attain the desired goals, etc. (1994, 116–117).

Changes are the basic process for a humanistic-existential understanding of a person. When Rogers talks about the structure of a personality, he constantly emphasizes its changing: "The best quality of life is that it is a process of a flow and changes, where nothing is determined in advance. I came to the conclusion (with my clients and with myself) that life is at its richest point and it gave us most satisfaction when we accept it as a process that flows. [...] Life is conducted by the understanding and interpretation of our own experiences, which are constantly changing. It is always in the process of making. I believe that now it is possible to understand why there is no philosophy, religion or group of principles that I could suggest to others and convince them to accept it. I can only try to live my interpretation of my present experience and let others develop their own internal image, which would enable them to interpret their own experience in a way that is logical to them." (Rogers 1995, 27).

---

[31] Here we are talking about taking into account three standpoint dimensions, strongly linked together: a cognitive one (behaviours, knowledge, experiences, information, arguments regarding an object, an event, a person, a situation of which we form a point of view), an emotional-qualitative one (positive or negative emotions and evaluation of something we have a position on – sympathy, regret, hatred, attraction, contempt, etc.), and an active one (an individual's readiness to operate in a certain way, regarding his point of view) (Ule 1994, 116–117).

Rogers does not believe in the existence of objective reality. He thinks that the only reality is the one noticed by an individual. He emphasizes that everything we know is what we notice and we try to test it in different ways. When we notice, and it seems to appear the same way by looking at it from various points of view, we take it for something real. (Rogers in Evans 1988). The phenomenological field determines a person's subjective reality.

The supposition of humanistic psychology is that the core of human nature is positive in its essence. "My experience tells me that people are positively oriented at their core. I discovered this truth while in contact with individuals, some of them had extremely disruptive problems, incredibly antisocial behaviour, and their emotions seemed abnormal." (Rogers 1995, 27). Rogers's opinion is that the positive orientation of a personality's nature is one of the greatest discoveries, which represents a revolutionary implication of a widely accepted point of view. "Religion, especially the protestant Christian tradition, brought into our culture the idea that man is basically a sinner and only a miracle can change his sinful nature. In psychology, Freud and his successors presented a convincing statement that the id, a person's basis, the unconscious nature primary composed by instincts, would lead to incest, murder and other criminal activities if only we would allow it an undisturbed fulfilment." (ibid, 91). According to Rogers, a person's internal essence is an organism in itself with its social nature, prone to self-preservation (ibid). He explains that this conviction is based on clinical experiences, when the client in a therapeutic process discovers the core of "self"— that represents a desire for a personal growth, a self-actualization. This tendency "[…] is present in a person's capacity to understand himself and the parts of his life that cause him pain and dissatisfaction. The mentioned tendency is present in the understanding which penetrates through an individual's conscious view of himself. It is present in the understanding of the experiences that an individual has hidden from himself because of their dangerous nature. It manifests itself in the tendency to re-organise one's personality and one's attitude towards life in order to become more mature. Regardless of how we name it, the tendency leaning toward progress, the instinct leading to self-realization, the tendency to a forward-oriented move, this is the primary origin of life. It is a strong impulse that is present in the whole organic and human life, an impulse to expand, become independent, to progress. It is a tendency to express and activate all of our organism's capacities to the point that the organism or "self" becomes stronger thanks to this activity. This tendency can be buried under layers of rigid psychological defences. It can be hidden under a perfective facade that denies its existence, but it remains present in every individual and waits for appropriate conditions to express and realize itself." (ibid, 35).

While attempting to achieve self-actualization, Rogers, Maslow and other humanistic authors refer to "organismic wisdom". This is supposed to be the organism's quality that instinctively knows what is good for it and what is not. The organismic valuation process is a process that varies, is oriented forward and it is based on evaluation norms for the people that are important to the individual (Rogers in Pescitelli 1996). This can lead to a uniformity, when the concept of oneself is in harmony (congruent) with an individual's actual characteristics and it can develop normally and in peace, realize its actual potentials or it can lead to disharmony (incongruity) with an actual state, when the environment does not approve of an individual's determined characteristics and the individual suppresses these characteristics, he tries to hide them from himself and others, with which he removes them from his self-image (Musek 1999). According to Rogers, it is possible to eliminate the incongruity between the image of oneself and the organismic tendencies with a non-selective, unconditional acceptance and positive evaluation of an individual. In doing so, we create a holistic and positive view of the individual's personality (Rogers 1995, 34).

Rogers believes that a fully functional person is someone who focuses on living in the present. "Living in the present moment represents the lack of rigidity, a strong organization, the absence of the forced shaping of experience into an existing structure. On the contrary, it means a maximal adaptability, discovering the structure within the experience, mobility and variability in organizing oneself and our own personality", he says (ibid, 188–189). He also linked the confidence in our own organism, creativity, and the experience of freedom to a successful realization of an actualising tendency. According to Rogers, a fully functional person, not only experiences, but also uses free choice when he chooses spontaneously, freely, and in good faith, which is absolutely determined. The individual chooses the activity direction, which is also the most economic vector in a relation to all internal and external tendencies, because that is the behaviour that offers the greatest satisfaction (ibid, 190, 193–194).

Based on the research and the clinical work, besides the theoretic viewpoints, Rogers also formed a psychotherapeutic approach[32] called "client-oriented therapy". With self-understanding, the changing of the "self" concept, one's own behaviour, and a self-oriented behaviour, an individual can turn into a fully functional person, but only after a determined experience in the relationship. With that, Rogers opposes creating any sorts of control, given that liberating oneself is the precondition for his turning into a fully functional person. Rogers's view of the relationship, which helps the individual to acquire a fully functional personality, does not work only for the therapist-client relationship, but also for relationships in society in general (ibid, 39–40).

The basis of humanistic psychology is the individual, his conscious motivation, and free will. This is why humanists locate the problem within the individual and not in society. For socially critical psychologists the phenomenological approach is unacceptable. Skinner

---

[32] Besides Rogers's indirective, client-oriented therapy, the humanistic paradigm also presents gestalt therapy (Fritz Perls), the transaction analysis (Eric Berne), logo therapy (Viktor E. Frankl), reality therapy (William Glasser) and others.

(1953), an objectively oriented psychologist, defended the conviction that human behaviour is overall the consequence of environmental influences and that is why a person cannot decide freely. Radical behaviourists are not interested in mental, introspective processes in the organism, because they believe those processes cannot be scientific objects, since they are not accessible to objective research.

Behaviourists believe that social relationships are the ones forming personalities and also preventing self-actualization, which could not be attained with individual improvement (Musek 1988). Meanwhile Maslow and Rogers emphasize self-actualization as an experiential principle and ethical idea (Friedman 1994).

Existentially oriented psychotherapy includes the humanistic paradigm of individuality, the complexity of mentality, the holistic-integral approach, free will and responsibility, the phenomenological approach, subjectivity besides objectivity, personal growth, self-actualization, and self-transcendence. It is characteristic of humanistic therapies to emphasize the stimulation of human capacities for experiencing emotions and thinking, and the activity within the capacities of every individual to realize himself as he is. Existential approaches to psychotherapy emphasize the individual's capacities to choose his own life situations.

THE REALITY PSYCHOTHERAPEUTIC
MODEL OF EXPLAINING
"PSYCHOPATHOLOGICAL" PHENOMENA

Reality therapy[33] is a consultative and therapeutic approach, developed by Glasser[34] on the basis of psychiatric practice and dissatisfaction with the (in)efficiency of the psychiatry of that time. In the early sixties, he gathered the ideas into the process of reality therapy. He later explained that process with the help of the Control Systems Theory by William Powers, upgraded his own theory and renamed it as Choice Theory (Zupančič 1997, 137).

Choice theory is quite similar in understanding human behaviours and practices to the phenomenological and existential orientations of humanistic psychology. The holistic and phenomenological orientation require that in the first place the person is treated first as a subject in his life situation, in his phenomenological and value dimensions, with his conscious experiences, assessments, goals, and emotions. We should not regard him as an object (behaviourism) or as a creature with an unconscious orientation (psychoanalysis) (Musek 2003, 212). It is also similar to humanism in its value of the human dignity. The therapist accepts and respects the human in all of his uniqueness and entity, and does not predict and control his behaviour, which is an instrument of external control psychology. An essential component of humanistic psychotherapy is the individualization and actualization of one's own goals, desires and the concretization and deepening of the authenticity of one's life. Through the experience of the relationship with the therapist, who believes that the behaviour is conditioned by a certain purpose, the client realizes that he is not an object but a subject of events, that he can always choose another, more effective behaviour in order to fulfil his own desires and needs. Therefore, from the choice

---

[33] Reality therapy is one of the top ten most-used psychotherapeutic methods in the world (Glasser 2007a).

[34] Glasser is one of the most famous psychiatrists who refuse to resort to solving mental health problems which have no organic proven causes with medicaments. He believes that mental health problems originate from a person's unsuccessful attempts to connect with others. This is why all the psychotherapeutic methods whose definition is based on relationships – regardless of the modality – focus on the aetiology of mental problems (Novak 2007, 11).

theory standpoint, the behaviour of an individual is not a mere response to circumstances, but an attempt to achieve an optimum consistency between his inner world of qualities and the outside world, as perceived (Glasser 1998).

Choice theory ranks reality therapy as a constructivist therapy, where mental health problems are not perceived as entities of individual diagnoses, nor ascribed to personality traits or as part of the personality development, but they are perceived as different, in the opinion of reality therapists, as very creative, sometimes very strange ways of exerting control over the environment, when perceived as extremely unfavourable (Lojk 2012, 111).

The advantages of reality therapy can be seen especially in its efficacy, the client's initiative and the development of his self-confidence, the responsibility for his behaviour, and with that the preservation of human dignity (Lojk and Lojk 2011, 327). The usefulness of reality therapy is successful with voluntary and non-voluntary clients. In its application, reality therapy has developed techniques that help to get from a confrontational conversation to a collaborating one (Lojk 2002). The basic thesis, that the critiques present as weaknesses of reality therapy, are rooted in the doubt that adequate relationships with other people is a solution for all mental problems, that the explanation of human behaviour with a different number of differently defined needs shows that mental needs are not scientifically proved, that the theory has too little emphasis on the past, it does not take into consideration the subconscious and subconscious conflicts,and can, while emphasizing the possibility of choosing and consequently the responsibility for one's own suffering, pass to blaming and moralising (Lojk and Lojk 2011, Wubbolding, 2000). The representatives of the reality approach identify its limits while working with people who at a very young age have lost contact with a responsible adult and, because of that, have difficulties finding satisfaction in relationships, even if they cannot give up on them. They search for satisfaction outside human relationships, in drugs, alcohol, sexual pleasure without love and in controlling others while inflicting pain on them (Lojk 2002). The limits of this method can be seen when the client does not accept the thesis that it is he who accepts the present behaviour and that he does not need to remain a victim of the past (ibid).

Regarding the approaches that explain pathological behaviour, Lojk (1998, 20, 21) defines reality therapy and choice therapy as the closest to the evolutionary-systematic approach, which developed with the occurrence of cybernetics and understands the behaviour of every life organism as an adjustment of external variables, which he tries to redesign in his favour while basing on past experiences and prior knowledge[35] (ibid). The evolutionary-systematic approach explains a person's strange behaviour as a creative attempt to control external variables, suiting an individual's "prior knowledge". He also does not explain

---

[35] The concept of prior knowledge includes experiences and an individual's knowledge, but mainly an evolutionary gained knowledge of the species (Lojk 1998).

any present behaviour as a consequence of external forces in the environment, but as a purposive exertion of adapting this force to his own internal criteria (ibid, 28).

Among the various approaches to the explanation of psychopathological behaviour, reality therapy being the closest one, is cognitive behaviourism. It is similar to reality therapy as it emphasizes activity and thinking as important factors of the client's changes, wherein reality therapy uses the overview and evaluation of the client's present behaviour, which usually is not successful. Reality therapy and rational emotive therapy have in common the belief that the past should not be too examined and that the present and future are the most important. Reality therapy distinguishes itself from Ellis's approach to the fact that human behaviour is understood as a choice and that it emphasizes more the active component of behaviour. Defending an indirect path in a process is common to reality therapy and the humanistic approach. Both originate from the belief that a person is a responsible being and that his behaviour is intentional (Lojk 1997, 8–9).

In choice theory, a person is understood as a free, responsible being who is intrinsically motivated and whose behaviour always follows a purpose, it is diverse and flexible (Glasser 2007). Reality therapy, based on the theological interpretation of human behaviour, also does not talk about "normal" and "psychopathological" behaviour and experience, but about an ineffective behaviour. It does not talk about psychopathological symptoms, but about painful forms of satisfying a person's needs that can even be dangerous to others. It also does not talk about a treatment as help and counselling. Besides the variety of their forms, according to Glasser, all those behaviours have only one purpose: reducing frustrations by satisfying the basic needs (in Lojk 2000).

The understanding of a person's phenomenological world in the context of choice theory brings an answer to the question of how a person should actualize himself within the given social possibilities that also include the risks that he is exposed to. The conviction of reality theory is that a person can always choose the behaviours that will successfully help him to satisfy his basic needs in the future, regardless of what is happening to him, will happen to him or what he has done until that moment (Glasser 2000). It represents a turn from understanding problems as mere consequences of external circumstances, the past or heredity to an understanding that describes problems as a less effective choice of behaviour.

The construct of individual differences of choice theory, individual choices of behaviour that individuals choose with different biological endowments and in different circumstances matches Adler's thought (1999) about the need to ask the question "How did a person take advantage of his heredity and the environment in order to become what he is?" and not "How do heredity and the environment influence what would a man become?"

The tendency to striving for self-actualization is based on the human motive, the quality world, to the realization for which a person strives all his life by choosing different, even destructive behaviours, in order to successfully satisfy his basic needs. By constantly choosing his behaviour, a person constantly discovers more satisfying ways of appeasing his needs. This behaviour could be very frustrating for him, because he tries constantly to get the real objective world closer to his idealized quality world with the most adequate behaviour (for which he believes that would help him appease his needs and reach a sense of comfort). From the point of view of creating the quality world, the social and cultural environment are essential for an individual's personal growth. The people that are part of an individual's quality world are extremely important, along with their behaviours and actions, the images and ways of appeasing their psychic needs because they contribute to co-creating the individual's internal quality world. In some way, the quality world is a construct of individual differences. Each choice or experience is marked with a human perspective from its origins. Individuals develop specific quality worlds based on individual behavioural choices with different biological endowments and in different circumstances. The question of self-activity is a component in our holistic behaviour that helps a person consciously build himself.

Here choice theory matches Berger and Luckmann's existential theory that "we could talk about human nature, but the fact that a person alone creates his nature, or more simply put, a person creates himself, it is more important" (Berger and Luckmann 1988, 53). The holistic and phenomenological orientation demand that a person is first a subject in his life situation, in his phenomenological and value dimensions, with his conscious experiences, judgments, goals and emotions. All we can give to or get from others is the information that the brain receives and processes, according to which an individual makes a decision (Glasser 2007a, 1). The subjective view and perception are an individual's conscious choice; they represent his internal control, personal responsibility[36] for the chosen behaviours and the best possibility to preserve the culture of relationships, and develop and keep the control over his life.

The basic existential concepts – sense, freedom, responsibility, individuality, authenticity, and choice – represent the basic constructs of the choice theory system and the psychotherapeutic reality approach.

The Theory of Personality

Glasser does not deliver a scientific explanation for researching a personality, which concerns the question of personal integration, personal structure, and personal dynamics, interpersonal differences, and personal growth. He defines the personality as a dominant

---

[36] It is not possible to talk about the choice of how to behave and responsibility in conditions of extreme poverty and diseases (Lojk, 2002).

form of behaviour with which a person establishes relationships with others in order to get the external, especially social world, as he experiences it closer to his desired ideas within his internal world (Glasser 2007a).

Glasser's theory of personality does not belong among theories that understand personality as a legitimate construct, hypothetical entity with its own role in causing and explaining behaviour (for example psychoanalysis, theory of types, and theory of moves) (Lojk 2012, 108). According to Lojk, Glasser's personality is secondary, deriving from the consistency of one's behaviour, where the causes of behaviour are found elsewhere, this is why a personality does not have an interpretative role (humanistic, behaviouristic, and some other theories do not have it as well) (ibid).

We can paradigmatically define choice theory and reality therapy constructively, because they do not acknowledge that an individual does not have the possibility to choose his goals and types of behaviour because of structural differences. Mental problems are not acknowledged as entities of individual diagnoses, neither do we attribute them to personal characteristics nor to personality development, but they understand them as various, destructive forms of control over the environment. The general tendency for self-actualization represents the basic dimension of personality in choice theory.

A postmodern view of the world signifies a passage from an objectivistic description of the world to a constructive one (Šugman Bohinc 2005, 3, 4). Through the objectivistic constructive epistemological glasses, the world treats an individual as a subject and every individual experiences the environment in his own way, which is under the influence of numerous factors. Besides the biological structure of senses and brains, we also have psychophysiological factors and psychosocial categories that a person gains while living in a determined time and space, in a defined culture, language, with a life and socialization in various contexts of social interaction (ibid, 5). A constructivism defined in such way could be also be called social constructivism, because it sees a person as a being who forms his own model of the world with the help of social representations or interactions among individuals. Therefore, a person is the constructor of reality and the product of constructions which are created through interactions among people (Musek 2003, 83).

The Construct of Basic Needs and the Motivational Construct

Choice theory originates from a holistic anthropological argument of an individual who appeases his existential needs as well as his psychic needs in a balanced way.

In his deepest essence, a person is a social and biological being, a creature of needs that drive him to realize himself as a person, who appeases his basic psychical needs in a satisfying way (by creating relationships with others), and by doing so he does not prevent others from appeasing their own basic needs. Glasser denies the Maslow's commonly established hierarchic structure of needs that states that a higher need appears when a lower one is appeased. He believes that "with the fact that we appease some of our genetic directives psychically and not physically, these directives are not less necessary and their origin is not les biological" (Glasser 2007, 9).

The group of basic needs has to be constantly satisfied and balanced, because according to Glasser, the motivation system is based on an internal origin of human behaviour. Besides survival, which depends on human physiology, an individual is also genetically programmed for an attempt to satisfy the basic psychic needs, "our genes motivate us for everything else, not only for our survival" (Glasser 2007a, 22), "our capacity, to start satisfying our needs even before we realize what we are doing it and why, is nature's real geniality" (ibid, 23), believes Glasser. The genetically determined needs represent a driving force that forces us into action.

Glasser (2007a) defines the need for love (acceptance, belonging, collaboration), power (validity, importance), freedom (independency, autonomy, creativity), and entertainment (discovering new things, changes, and playfulness) as basic and universal psychic needs. They are being taken care of by the centres in the newest parts of the brain, especially those in the cerebral cortex. Those needs are being realized through an individual's activity and while in touch with other persons (Zupančič 1997, 135). They are of vital importance for an individual, regarding the place in a person's genetic code (ibid). According to Glasser (in Zupančič 2007, 135), they need to be appeased daily at least on a minimal base in order to lead a quality life. A successful appeasement of needs is expressed through a sense of contentment, in the realization that the individual can control the world, and in the improvement of one's self-image and positive identity (Glasser 2007a). Symptomatic behaviours, on the other hand, are merely the organism's attempt to lower the frustration a client develops when he cannot appease his basic needs. His creative system therefore offers solutions with various emotional and physiological behaviours (ibid).

The evolutionary biologist Dawkins believes that "[…] we can rightly talk about a specific 'gene for a determined behaviour', even though we do not have the slightest idea of the chemical causal link that goes from the gene to the expressed behaviour." (Dawkins 2006, 86) "A lot of people risk or they even lose their life while trying to appease their needs for love, amusement, freedom, honour." (Lojk 2007, 238). Every choice we make leads to the appeasement of one or more genetic needs.

Geneticists are still trying to discover the true purpose of all hundreds of thousands of genes in the human genome. Glasser believes that "some of these unknown genes represent the basis of psychology – how we behave and what we decide to do with our life." (Glasser 2007a, 22). Despite the belief that human behaviour is based on the genetic code, Dawkins and the founder of socio-biology, Wilson, are not "genetic determinists" (Dawkins 2006, 383), but they predict that "genes can have a statistic influence on human behaviour and we can influence that in various ways and change it. Genes statistically influence each behaviour, which has developed through natural selection." (ibid). According to Dawkins, our brains are "separated" and "independent from our genes" (ibid) enough to let us make our own decisions.

A person is therefore a being of choice. The genes merely form the instructions that should be followed in order to survive and lead a satisfying life. "A lot of those instructions transform into images in our head and those have to be appeased through our way of life" (Glasser 1994, xiii). The images represent an individual's quality world, which a human being develops through a biological development, experiences, and creativity. While growing up, the content of the quality world gets richer, and the behaviours for appeasing needs become more and more varied.

The concept of choice is connected to the concept of responsibility. In choice theory, responsibility represents a behaviour and life which helps a person appease his basic psychic needs and at the same time, allows others to do the same (Glasser 2007a). The freedom of an individual's choice is limited by the responsibility towards himself and someone else. A chosen behaviour should not interfere with someone else's freedom. It is the only way it could be really effective and appeasing.

The Construct of the Quality World

The collection of good experiences, which appease an individual's needs, and represent a desired, personal, internal world, Glasser defines as the quality world (Glasser 1998, 55). An individual's quality world includes his most important discoveries, loved ones, things that he has or loves to experience, and various ideas and beliefs systems (ibid). The whole spectrum of these specific images, which represents the best ways of appeasing one or more basic needs, regulates most of an individual's behaviour, because he tries to change the real world in which he lives through all his life with activities, thoughts, and physical processes into a world that resembles his personal quality world (ibid, 58).

A person operates as a control system with the intention to realize the images from his quality world with which he satisfies his needs (Glasser 2007, 42). External information enters the "sensed world" through three filters: the sensorial filter, the filter of knowledge[37], and the filter of values.[38] By receiving information and while experiencing things, he valuates the real world. When information enters through the perception system, the sensorial cameras determine everything as good or bad. If a person does not interfere consciously, it happens quickly, automatically, and without him realizing it (ibid, 78). An individual's sensorial camera captures images of the world as he would like to see them, which is the closest thing to the images of his quality world (ibid, 80). In the background of our sensorial cameras, behind the collection of values, there is a valuation system, which is the final filter through which goes everything a person experiences (ibid, 83).

The perception is compared to the images of the world of desires. The findings that originate from this influence the behaviour that arose. The error signal activates a behaviour, which is oriented toward controlling the environment, in order to lower the difference. If the organism does not succeed, the tension remains and there is a search for new and more effective selections. First he uses all known paths and then he forms new ones. These new behaviours are not always better, more constrictive, and responsible. Better and more responsible responses need to be learned. The selections that better appease the needs on a long-term scale enable the increase of self-confidence, self-esteem, and positive identity. The contrary also stands. With bad selections, the dissatisfaction with oneself, with the surroundings, and one's own negative identity increases (Lojk 2007).

The developmental dimensions of a human being help a person discover new behaviours and develop new images in the quality world (images, desires), which are available

---

[37] The filter of knowledge is in the first part of our perceiving system. Here a person recognizes the known from the unknown or the experiences that he names. Every knowledge world includes images and memories of everything he has already experienced, regardless of whether the experiences were positive or negative. It is a memory of favourable or inconvenient, desired or undesired experiences, a memory of people, places, events, of all images that have a meaning for him. When a sense goes through this filter, it changes from sense to experience, a person notices that it is worthy of his attention. The perception is always in line with an experience he has already had. There are three possible ways of action: (1) he can recognize what it is and realize that it has a meaning for him; (2) he may not recognize what it is, but he wants to know, because he believes it could mean something to him; (3) he could recognize it or not, but he concludes that it does not have a meaning for him. In the next case this perception ends, everything that he recognizes or wants to discover passes through the next filter, the filter of values (Wubbolding 2000, 25–26).

[38] With the filter of values, a person evaluates his experience with a positive, negative, or neutral sign. This filter includes images of everything from his internal world. Here the perception is compared with images from the quality world and the findings that form here influence his behaviour. There is a comparison of what he knows or wants to discover, with the images from his quality world that appease his needs. If the things he perceives while they pass through the filter of values match with what he expects, he gives this perception a positive value. In the case the perception is contrary to his desires and expectations, he gives it a negative sign. It could happen that the perception is neither in line with his desires nor contrary to them. In this case he gives the perception a neutral value. This means that those perceptions remain the same as they were before passing through this filter (Wubbolding 2000, 27–28).

for appeasing needs. The manner of accepting and perceiving information builds an individual's real world and reflects his personal quality world.

The source of conflicts in personal relationships is the diversity of their personal worlds. The incompatibility of an individual's desired world with the real world creates the so-called internal conflict. While confronting a difficult frustration, an individual can, by making wrong choices (especially with emotional behaviour), be the sole one to choose most of his sufferings in his everyday life, even though he is not aware of it. He beliefs that this is the best attempt to regain control over his life (Glasser 1998, 70).

Glasser (2007a, 41) warns that for a satisfying appeasement of psychic needs in the quality world, objects, beliefs, and values are not enough. It is necessary to have people to connect with, who help the individual appease his psychic needs. People can change the images of their loved ones, for a momentary satisfaction, with a satisfaction without people, for various reasons (abuse, rejection, disappointment, etc.). These new images represent images of violence, drugs and sexuality without love (ibid). Those irrational images in a quality world endanger the life and health of people.

Most people keep the images in their quality world long after they are not capable of appeasing them anymore, and to a point they would want to appease them (ibid). The reasons for insisting on existing contacts are the fact that a person does not believe that a new image will satisfy him to the same measure as the existing one, and that he is not capable of renouncing the hope that he will eventually discover a new form of behaviour, with which he will attain what he desires (Glasser 2007, 33).

The quality world is not unchanging. It is possible to create and change it through life. When an image we have been keeping in our album is no longer as satisfying as we would want it to be, we tend to change it and start to search for new and more satisfying ones (ibid, 22). The images that are so important for us are difficult to substitute, because they are linked to positive emotions that we experienced when this image was appeasing our need. We cannot push images out of our consciousness, unless we substitute them with new ones. The new image has to appease the same need with equal success or effectiveness as the existing one.

Holistic Behaviour: Correlation Between Physicality and Mentality

A person tries to appease his basic needs with a holistic, indivisible behaviour. The concept of holistic, flexible, and creative[39] behaviour is a belief about the indivisibility of

---

[39] The concept of creative behaviour is needed for understanding an individual's human capacities of behaving destructively if his life is in danger or he had not appeased his basic needs in a long time (Lojk and Lojk 2011).

physicality and mentality. A person's physical activity, thinking, emotions, and physiological phenomena represent four components of a behaviour a person uses to "change the real world as he experiences it into a world which resembles his personal quality world." (Lojk and Lojk 2011, 314).

A person tries to appease the long-time unsatisfied basic needs with a rigid repetition of an ineffective behaviour or with a new, reorganized, creative behaviour, which is equally ineffective and destructive (ibid, 315), but on purpose – it offers him at least some control over the appeasing of his needs (ibid, 316).

Choice theory substantiates the reorganization of behaviour[40] – the phenomenon of mental health problems and other forms of destructive physiology (autoimmune and other psychosomatic illnesses) – with the use and/or participation of the external control. Besides choice theory, which distinguishes itself from neo-behaviourism with a theological explanation of the human personality, Powers' biologically perceptive control theory (2005) with a systematic-cybernetic model also explains the behaviour of living organisms with natural technology. Powers, understanding human behaviour, has defined, based on the experiments of second-class cybernetics[41] the variables that a person can control. To supervise, to control does not mean responding to a stimulus as it is described in the theory of behaviourism, which also pushes the processes in the organism between the stimulus and the reaction and, by doing so, it explains the differences in people's behaviours. Control theory and choice theory explain the blank in the causal-consecutive reaction with human beings' expedience behaviour. This way, the stimulus does not determine the behaviour, it merely mediates the information (in reality therapy – where and how to satisfy the basic needs), but it cannot define the choice of behaviour (considering the integral behaviour and not the feelings and physiological processes) or other ways of constraint. In an individual's autonomy, the behaviour is in line with the purpose that he wants to attain. The action outside the organism is not a stimulus that causes the organism's reactions, but a disorder,[42] controlled by the organism.

From the point of view of a holistic definition of behaviour, choice theory supposes that by changing one component, the thinking one or active one, the other two components are subjected to physiological and emotional changes. Based on the simultaneous activity of all four components of holistic behaviour, Glasser defines the possibility of choice and indirectly also a stricken behaviour. "The idea that you always try to choose the best

---

[40] Glasser treats mental health problems as behaviour problems and not as a mental disorder or illness.

[41] Second-class cybernetics studies systems that study other systems, while first-class cybernetics studies the human relation with the system, but it doesn't originate from the phenomenological perspective of understanding the systematic theory of oneself.

[42] The disorders are represented by the discordance between the perception of reality and the desired state of the organism.

option of a given moment is essential for the understanding of holistic behaviour." (Glasser 1998, 82). "With that the efficacy of behaviour changes, and the possibility of a better appeasement of the basic psychic needs increases" (Zupančič, 1997, 137), as the possibility to influence the physical, mental, and social health (Lojk 2012, 109).

The Therapist–Client Relationship

The formation of the therapeutic culture, which marked the second half of the 20th century, was strongly influenced by Rogers, who transformed the basis of the directive medical model of the relationship between the patient and the doctor. Moreover, he explained client-oriented humanistic theory, which enables the client to self-actualize and leads to a formation of a personality as a whole (Evans 1975).

At a first look, reality therapy differs from Rogers's person-oriented therapy, which emphasizes emotions, reflective listening, the self-initiative that the client takes and starts talking, and the consideration of his own decisions for a change (Zupančič 1997, 143). Reality therapy gives priority to an active approach, to questions, which orient a client to realize the effectiveness of his behaviour up to this point, and to the search for a more effective one (ibid). Besides all that, both therapies have in common the belief in the good of human nature, the human personal responsibility towards people, the logic of behaviour and both attribute a great importance to trust and authenticity (ibid).

The real (Rogers, Glasser), supportive, empathic, and at the same time honest and direct (but not directive) relationship creates a safe, trusting counselling atmosphere, which enables the client to successfully appease his needs in the relationship with the therapist. This is why a responsible personal connection between the counsellor and the client is the best, the fastest, and frequently the only way to teach the client how to develop relationships with people he needs (Lojk 2002, 8).

The relationship between a therapist and a client is extremely important in reality therapy. The therapist can be the only person that can help the client to appease his basic needs in a better and more responsible way, (Zupančič 1997, 138) and to acquire the opportunity to learn a more suitable way of developing good relationships with his loved ones. A mutual relationship emerges, which helps the therapist to successfully appease his psychic needs too, and consequently allows him to establish a satisfying relationship with the client. This further allows the opportunity for self-reflection and to acquire new images for appeasing his needs.

The therapist develops with the client a relationship of mutual understanding and respect, a friendly atmosphere, and an authentic contact (ibid), which helps to "create open spaces for a discussion that enable a dialogue and the co-creation of new stories" (Čačinovič Vogrinčič 2000, 83). Postmodernism emphasises the question of the relationship among the people taking part in the therapy and the counselling. It redefines the processes of discussion, communication and response, thus making the relationship between the counsellor and the client extremely important (ibid, 86).

THE PSYCHOTHERAPEUTIC AND SOCIAL-ANTHROPOLOGICAL ANALYSIS OF PSYCHIC CRISES

In the empirical research field of the monograph we orientate from pathogenesis (the understanding of the creation and the development of mental health problems) towards salutogenesis, towards regaining mental health. The objectives of this discussion reach further from the findings on how social factors influence an individual and what consequences they bring to his mental health. The same objectives also surpass the theory of illness, studying from the viewpoint of various explanation models of "psychopathological" phenomena.

We approach the treatment of mental problems with the concept of understanding reality psychotherapy, explained by choice therapy. The chosen psychotherapeutic modality is "internationally accepted as an effective form of treatment" (Lynch in Glasser 2003, 5) and I have been using it in my work for fifteen years, almost from the beginning of my professional sessions with "unhappy" people. Those people include children and adolescents with learning disorders, labelled as "problematic", "hyperactive", with an "attention disorder", numerous partners, spouses who tried to save their marriage or decided to separate, and even on the shards of their marriage, they tried to regain control over their lives with various controlling ways (with which they destroyed their marriage). In individual or group therapeutic work that includes people with mental health problems, I constantly hear stories of painful relationships, injustices, unfulfilled expectations, unappeased desires and yearnings, numerous attempts to change the other, the experience of how others tried to change them, and how painful these experiences have been.

It seems no one can escape external control.

Universal psychology, based on the concept of behaviourism, has kept its power in all human relationships and social systems. It is strongly rooted in an individual's consciousness. It strongly influences modern, and especially Western society, to which social isolation, alienation from oneself and others, are immanent. The psychology of control, punishment, with the destruction of personal freedom, is a source of dissatisfying relationships, which damage other people's lives.

The basis of erroneous beliefs in external control psychology is the fact that a person is externally motivated and that it is possible to control him with means of control and constraint. These controlling behaviours create hard frustrations within an individual, which he tries to alleviate with unsuitable and especially with emotional behaviours, believing that it is the best way to make himself feel better.

A dissatisfying appeasing of psychic needs manifests itself in the modern person's everyday reality in numerous, destructive ways, depending on the creativity of the brain. We included some of them in the empirical research area of the present monograph. We will analyse five frequent types of behaviour in the form of a case study, and we will interpret them with the use of choice theory. We chose it as an interpretative tool for the explanation of the origin of psychic crises and it will lead us to the answer to how a person should act and behave in order to keep or regain mental health, despite his biological endowment and his position in a defined socio-cultural environment.

With this research, we want to show to what extent it is possible to support the theoretical observations and predictions about the prospects for resolving the problems in mental health with the selected psychotherapeutic approach. In this, the plurality of the presented case studies will enable the identification of the repetition of certain features and consolidate the perception of the predicted patterns.

The purpose of the research work is not simply to agree with the chosen theory. A sufficiently open conceptual framework within the theoretical part allows us to produce a starting point for a comprehensive understanding of the human being and improve general psychotherapy practices with the use of a methodological analysis of the collected material.

The analysis of the material was realized in accordance with the basic procedures in the grounded theory, also named inductive theory (Mesec, 1998, 33). The distinction of this theory is the theoretical sampling – it is an intentional assortment of units that contributes to further development of the theory on the basis of previous knowledge and of acquired data during numerous analyses. With an accurate definition of the content characteristic of defined phenomena, we determined the notions that represented the conditions in which activities and interactions appear, where these phenomena express themselves, and the consequences that they cause. By coding the data, we opened the data for an analytical proceeding, defined the concepts, their characteristics and dimensions, and we installed them into the context. Furthermore, we linked them together and combined them in concepts of a higher level and category. Through the method of constant comparison, we searched for similarities and differences, and for particularities of individual phenomena, developed generative questions, and formed ad hoc hypotheses. We simultaneously examined the hypothesis in the data, annotated analytical notes (*memos*) that are used for supporting the process of data analysing, and later we used them as a description of theoretical cognitions (Struebing v Kavčič 2011, 35, 36). We followed the basic task of grounding theory, i.e. the research of connections. We turned towards searching for common points of different problems and 'diagnoses' in the area of mental health, we studied the factors that have an influence on the manifestation of psychic crises, the characteristics of an individual's consideration and activity, and the larger socio-cultural context of psychic crises manifestation and treatment.

The presented work with clients ranks among the case studies because it is in fact an exploration of a coherent world of events in a social entity. Its analysis led us to the discovery of patterns of conduct that may be, just on the basis of a single case, linked to a particular behavioural strategy. At the same time, our case study provides us an insight into the conditions under which such a strategy was developed. We investigate several cases, perform plural studies, so that, by repeating the observations and findings, further studies of various cases enable us to make connections between concepts and strengthen the existence of the strategy and their interaction with the context.

We concluded the analysis with the formulation of a theory, a contextually bounded theory, which represents a reflection of observations, considerations, deductions, regularities, legalities, typologies, etc., of an individual's forms of behaviour, acts, convictions, at which we took into consideration the psychotherapeutic, psychosocial, and socio-anthropological aspect.

The analysis of case studies was performed by means of the ATLAS.ti[43] program for processing qualitative data. The program was used as an expedient for the technical facilitation of the coding proceedings, the development of concepts and their connection into larger units, and for establishing correlations among the units. We added the newly formed proper relations to the network of relations that are automatically formed by the program, and in this way we embraced all the recognized relations in the analyzed text.

---

[43] The Atlas.ti program was used to codify by marking the chosen citations and annotating the categories (codes) and units (families). In this book, I created concepts, connected them with the tool 'networks' to each other and united them into units that I had previously defined. The program also enables the noting down of analytical notes (*memos*), which were of help when writing the final interpretations. The procedures were performed on the whole hermeneutic unit or on the primary document (case studies).

The Case Study: the Reality Psychotherapeutic Approach to the Treatment of Psychic Crises

There were five examples of destructive forms of manifesting dissatisfaction included into the research – mental health problems, psychosomatic problems, obsessive thoughts and compulsive behaviour, sexual addiction, and difficulties in growing up. The only criterion in choosing the cases from the psychotherapeutic approach was the fact that they belong to different problematic areas, so the variety of the problems helps to connect with the characteristics and conduction of the psychotherapeutic process in case of different psychic crises. The chosen case studies represent individual and partner counselling-therapeutic work, therapeutic work with an adolescent and his parents (parallel), and work with adults, who have problems establishing and regaining an effective control over their lives.

The case study[44] represents the client's story and their interpretation of the problems, the therapist's understanding of the client's problems through the concepts of the choice theory, a summary of parts of the conversation that are important for the reestablishment of the relationship, for discovering the client's world of qualities, for understanding the client's endeavours, and for the client's shifting from the convictions of psychology of external control to the convictions of the choice therapy. The case study also includes the record of the therapist's internal dialogue and his professional inclusion (the therapist mediates the knowledge of choice theory to the client. Ultimately the practical work is a review of the amelioration of mental health through the study of choice theory and that has an important contribution to an individual's autonomy, a necessary independence from the therapist.

Qualitative case studies[45] with a deep insight into the socio-psychological reality of a chosen group of people represent at the same time the process itself – the case study includes at least six sessions with the client, which means that he was observed for at least three months, in most cases, for a year.

Mental health problems

The demonstration of the case of mental health problems represents psychotherapeutic treatment in line with the hypothesis of basic needs in reality therapy, i.e. the people who embark on treatment cannot develop adequate relationships with others, they do not successfully appease their basic needs, or they do appease them in ways that obstruct

---

[44] The text is published with the clients permission.
[45] The case studies are supervised, adequate, and in line with the chosen psychotherapeutic concepts from a psychotherapeutic viewpoint.

others from appeasing theirs. The presented study is an example of developing adequate relationships in order to achieve mental health.

Vid is a little over fifty years of age. He lives with his parents and so does his younger brother. He describes his mother as a severe, direct woman and his father as the mother's opposite, quiet and adapting, submissive to the wife. From the client's presentation of his family I conclude that his father tries as best as he can with his own choosing to contribute to the preservation of the marriage and the family. I do not have any information about his health, therefore I can only assume that in a relationship where he experiences external control, it is difficult for him to appease his basic psychic needs. Like both children, who are already adults but not prepared for an independent life, Vid's father is also constantly criticized, insulted, underestimated, and mocked. Therefore, no one appease his own psychic needs in a satisfying way in his relationship with the loved person, mother/wife. According to Vid's description, the mother doesn't show her love through her language but by expressing concern (and not with the desired attention, showing of love, which Vid missed in their relationship) that everything is as it must be. By following this objective, she followed her image of how she looks and what a good mother does – controls, orders, with the intention of making the children do and become what she perceives as her quality world.

Vid and his brother tried, each in his way, to appease their unsatisfied needs in a destructive way.

For several years Vid's brother searched in alcohol for the sense of happiness, satisfaction, acceptance, importance, the ability to choose freely, the possibility to decide, and the ability to manage his life as he deems. Vid chose the worse way, to suffer and dwell in depression. For him depression represented a way out of his mother's regime, as he calls her behaviour. The "illness" was a good excuse not to have to constantly obey his mother's orders; this state also helped him to have some control over his mother. He ensured for himself, in a hurtful way, hours of lying in bed without having anyone bothering him, giving him orders, and telling him that "he is no good for anything".

Vid talked about his mother mocking the culture and art that he loved, and which represent his quality world. His mother appreciates and expects from all hard physical work at home and on the family-owned land, with no possibilities of going out with friends, sports activities, and art. Vid's and his mother's quality world are clearly very different.

I think Vid's stammering, that started at a young age, is connected to the fact that he has been exposed to external control psychology since he was a child. His stammering brought further criticism from his mother, because she could not accept it. So, she tried to eliminate it unsuccessfully and in a destructive way by criticising and controlling him.

Vid also said that no girl he or his brother brought home fulfilled their mother's expectations. Today they are both adults and still single, they could not create a relationship or live with a partner. Despite her old age, their mother still takes care of their food, clothes, etc. This may be her image of a good mother (to be attentive), her "language of love", with which she tries to appease her needs and preserve her health. But I believe that she does not feel good, because her behaviour ("Our mother is direct, she always tells people what she thinks to their faces," Vid describes her) has contributed to numerous destroyed relationships, not only within the family. For years Vid's family has been on bad terms with their neighbours and his father's relatives. Vid accepted this with great difficulty since it meant that he was not part of the village society and therefore deprived of another possibility to appease his psychic needs.

Vid regularly visits the psychiatrist and takes antidepressants. In September 2008, he started attending training sessions for improving social skills at Association for Mental Health. He was in distress; we agreed on an individual conversation.

He expressed the desire to come to me, because he is not satisfied with his life. He told me that he was deprived of many things in his life, therefore he could not realize the images he was following in his life. He had a strong desire to become a priest, but his parents did not approve of this. Even today, when his mother sees him reading books, she tells him angrily to go to a monastery. His mother's mocking hurts him, because it makes him think that what he does is not right, it is not good enough for his parents.

He decided to study, to become a toolmaker and he worked as such, but during all his working years he was very unhappy. At work, as at home, he could not appease his need for freedom, amusement, power. He did not pursue his interest in music, art, literature, philosophy, etc., and thus he remained frustrated.

In my role of therapist, I saw the possibility to connect with the client through the various activities that interest him. I asked him about him and his interests (playing the guitar, writing poems, playing chess, listening to music, etc.), I supported and encouraged him. I think that we have established a confidential and connecting relationship, which contributed to his learning process and to the realization of his image.

I saw in the client a distinct unsatisfied need for power. At home, he still gets messages that he is lazy, that he does not deserve retirement, that what he does is not even work. He feels unaccepted and unappreciated as he is. With the help of messages that came from others (you are clumsy, lazy, not good, etc.), he formed beliefs, even about himself. This is why I listened carefully to the client, I asked him questions, I showed interest in his knowledge so that he helped me establish a connection with him, and helped him to appease his need for power and acceptance in the relationship he and I shared. Since my behaviour was real, I learned a lot from Vid, he taught me much about history and the great thinkers, besides the importance of good relationships for our health and a satisfying life. I believe Vid helped himself the most, especially with the activities he introduced into his life. He just needed more support for him to change his beliefs and in giving up control.

I believe that, in my role as counsellor, I enabled him to have a good relationship in which he was able to realize what his family thought to be "forbidden", "unwanted", and even "condemned". He had my support in doing what he liked and for the first time he decided himself (and not his mother or anyone else in his place), he let himself be the adult Vid.

I present one of the discussions about the client's vision and experience of his mother's behaviour.

T: Vid, you said that yesterday you had another fight with your mother. Do you want to talk about it?

K: Yes, because it was a completely normal fight, something that keeps constantly repeating itself, because my mother cannot understand that I need time for myself. She wants me to work all day, she is constantly giving me orders.

T: What did you want to do?

K: I wanted to spend the afternoon reading a book. To be alone with myself, in peace.

T: Did you have time for yourself?

K: Not at all, she had to get her way.

T: You say that your mother constantly gives you orders. You have mentioned that quite a few times. Can you tell me more about this situation?

K: She has a plan in her mind, regarding what needs to be done that day and she does not deviate from that, not for a second. When everything is done, she is extremely satisfied, you can really see how satisfied she is. But I am nervous, because there is no time for my things, my brother is also nervous, our father is used to this.

T: It can't be easy for him either.

K: No, it is not, he just doesn't say anything anymore, he's silent, but my brother and I, we try to resist.

According to what he told me, I imagine that he does not have a good relationship with his mother, but I wanted the client to make an estimation of their relationship. Furthermore, I wanted us both to find some good parts of their relationship that could help us search for new and more successful ways of appeasing their mutual needs during the next sessions. I think it is important, since it is an important relationship for the client – it is a relationship with his mother, and because of her exerting external control psychology, there are surely very important but unappeased needs in their relationship.

Therefore, the question in front of us is: how could Vid appease his basic psychic needs in the presented relationship, if he could see and understand his mother differently, through the beliefs of choice theory. By changing the perception of his mother, he could consequently choose the behaviours he would use to connect with her.

Further on I will take into consideration what the client said and I will try to follow the thoughts mentioned above.

T: Vid, you came searching for help and you want some changes in your life, so we will focus on you. Do you agree?

K: I agree, of course.

T: Good. Would you please try to describe the relationship you have with your mother?

K: To me it doesn't seem very good, but maybe she thinks that we get along well, that as mother and son we make a good team.

T: We can only guess how your mother experiences this relationship, because she's the only one who knows her opinion. I'm interested in your vision of the relationship. What do you feel towards your mother?

K: In my opinion, it's not a good relationship. To me, my mother seems like a cop, her behaviour reminds me of the time I spent in the army, constantly under control and obeying orders. It makes me crazy! No one can stand her dictatorship.

T: If we understand this as a dictatorship and a limitation of your personal freedom, then we surely can't feel good.

K: What else could it be if not terror? She's been like this since I can remember! Why does she do that?

T: I believe that she follows her objectives and it all comes from her. Maybe she doesn't know how to act differently, maybe it's her way of expressing concern for her three men. Do you believe you could think of it like this?

K: The fact that she is an attentive mother and wife is indisputable. She's even too attentive. Everything is washed, ironed, cooked. There's no doubt about it. She's a hardworking woman, but she doesn't show her emotions. I miss that in her. If only she had said sometimes: How are you Vid, are you alright? I don't hear that.

T: She probably expresses this concern for you in some other way.

K: Maybe by knowing everything I do. By constantly controlling me and not letting me go anywhere.

The client has a strong belief that his behaviour depends on his mother's and he has been reinforcing this belief all his life. He perceives his mother as someone who has the strength to manage him. This is why he feels trapped in the relationship with his mother. He beliefs that he has no control over his behaviour. Further on, I will try to lead the discussion so that the client abandons his role of victim and reaches personal freedom by changing the perception of his mother's behaviour.

T: It is possible. Also, the fact that she takes care of your food, clothes, etc., as you said. Could you understand her behaviour as concern?

K: I could but her control over me still bothers me.

T: How do you normally react to this control?

K: With anger, screaming, blaming, insulting. I tell her everything. I just explode. I can't stand it anymore.

The client's face became red, he clenched his hands into fists and gritted his teeth. That, what he was merely thinking about during our discussion was showing also on his body and emotions, and all of it is in line with the understanding of the holistic behaviour. There was an extremely angry man in front of me. Anger caused by the helplessness he felt, because he doesn't know how to control his reactions in similar situations, he does not have the sense of control over his behaviour. By believing in external control theory, it is difficult for him to control his behaviour.

T: I understand that it is difficult to control oneself under such pressure and that it is difficult to withstand the kind of pressure that you are exposed to. I can also see that it upsets you and it does not do you any good.

K: Of course not! My blood pressure went through the roof, I'm so upset that I smoke one cigarette after another even two hours after a fight and I need quite a while to calm down.

T: Yes, it's true that bad relationships affect our mental and physical health. Have you ever thought about choosing another type of behaviour in the relationship with your mother when she gives you orders? Something that wouldn't make you upset and wouldn't hurt you.

K: I remember that for some time I practiced the: "Yes, mum", "I understand, mum", "You're right, mum" approach. Like in the army (laugh).

T: And how did it work?

K: Good. We didn't have any fights because she always got her way.

T: But is today any different? She still gets her way, as you say.

K: Yes, she still gets her way. I can't win and get my way.

T: What prevents you from getting your way, as you said?

K: Well, my mother, who else!

T: How would you feel if you were to behave in opposition to your mother's expectations, if you were to behave your way?

K: I think that would be even worse. She would think that I was teasing her on purpose.

T: How would you feel in this case?

K: I think that in a way I'd feel like had won, like I did it. On the other hand, I'd know that I had disappointed her.

T: Disappointed?

K: Because I didn't obey her. I believe it's better to obey her, if I want to have any peace, since it doesn't help me at all to just explode. At the moment I'm not ready to contradict her.

T: Do you think that you could, just for starters, try what you have already practiced, meaning agreeing with her, and meanwhile we could try to find better ways to appease your needs?

K: I don't know if it would work, last time I had just come from the mental institution and I was under a heavy dose of medication.

T: You said that now you're still taking medication, if this thinking helps you. But regardless of the drugs, it is about the choice of behaviour, your choice, of how you want to behave. You said that getting upset harms you and that you'd prefer to feel at peace. And you learn how to do that. Would you try to use this method until our meeting next week?

K: I will, if it is possible.

T: Concentrate on yourself, on your behaviour, on what is good for you. Next time we will try to decide how you could take care of yourself, of your needs, while trying to assure your peace.

At our next session, we continued the discussion by first talking briefly about the book he had been reading and then I checked how successful he had been in abandoning the external control over his mother (the screaming, insulting, anger, etc.) and connecting with her in the past week.

T: Vid, we concluded our last discussion agreeing that you'd try to react differently to your mother's ways of exerting control over you, in order to feel better. How did it go?

K: I'm quite satisfied. I have to say that I didn't get upset so much, I was very calm.

T: Could you say that in that time you got along with your mother a little more?

K: Maybe a little. We didn't fight, that's true, but we weren't close either.

T: Was it better than normally?

K: Yes, it was.

T: In your opinion, what could bring you closer to your mother? What do you share with her, what do you have in common?

K: I think she loves books too, it's just that she doesn't read them, so it wouldn't be my way.

T: I thought that maybe she doesn't have time to read, given the fact that she has so much work to do.

K: Yes, yes, that too. But she won't take any time to read, since there are so many more "better" things to do, as she says.

T: We frequently search for reasons for other people's behaviour in ourselves, as they try to do something to us, to hurt us or anything else with their behaviour, while they basically try just to appease their needs with their behaviour. You mentioned that your mother is also interested in books.

K: Yes, sometimes I tell her that she could also read, that it wouldn't hurt her. That makes her extremely angry, she becomes furious.

T: So it seems that this wasn't a good way of connecting with her.

K: No. She gets very angry.

T: Have you maybe talked with her about what you read? I'm thinking that it could interest her, but she doesn't have the time to read about it herself.

K: Sometimes I tell her something, briefly, because I get the feeling that she's not interested in what I read. She likes poetry. Maybe I could read her a poem sometimes.

T: Would you? Would that make you happy?

K: It would. Why not? I like reading to others, here in the Day center too, I'll just do that for her too.

T: Good. Maybe this could get you closer. Maybe this way she could understand you better, what reading means to you. You'll see how it goes. If necessary, we could return to the relationship with your mother.

An important shift that I perceived in the client, is the change of believing in what he does. Not only did he start to accept himself as he is, but he also started to value himself and believe that what he does is good, that his capacity for learning, remembering (reciting a poem by heart, quoting the thoughts of philosophers, etc.) is a quality, that not everyone knows how to play a guitar and also that a good game of chess demands a certain knowledge and skills. During his "revival" of interest activities, I encouraged him, supported him, and we planned attentively all the activities together. It seems that Vid does not have problems with doing that, since these are areas that interest him very much. The problem was in the voice that was always present in the back of Vid's consciousness – what would my mother say, my mother would go mad, she will throw me out of the house, etc. Vid perceives himself as a child without power and value. Of course, we could not predict his mother's reaction, but according to his past experiences and knowing his mother very well, Vid could guess how she would behave. Besides, he worried over the belief that his parents might understand his new activities the wrong way, as a "worsening of his health". In case of such a scenario, we prepared an additional plan of possible behaviours. In the beginning, he talked with his mother about what he wants to do in the future (to read more, play guitar, to take walks in nature, and help at home), he showed her how much it all means to him, and that this is the source of his happiness and satisfaction. Since Vid knows his mother's quality world and her infinite value of hard work and carrying out "duties", we decided that he should discuss with his mother his contribution to the household chores. After doing so, they agreed that he would help with the preparation and regular bringing of the wood. Vid found this acceptable; he thinks it is right to contribute to the shared household of the family.

Further on, I will present the discussion leading to abandoning control and searching for new possibilities to get the client closer to his mother. The client will also judge the efficacy of the activities and new behaviours he introduced into his life during the therapy.

[...]

T: If reading books makes you happy, along with everything else you described, from painting to going to concerts, I don't see why you shouldn't do those things.

K: I think that too, but my mother wouldn't agree with that, she doesn't respect art.

T: It's not completely true, since you told me that she likes poetry. But your belief is much more important, because you don't have the power, and neither do I, to change your mother's belief.

K: Now I realize that I have a lot of qualities, that I'm skilled, but in my family that was always questionable, this is why I was laughed at, felt worthless. So, after some years I started to believe that playing the guitar wasn't enough, that reading and painting weren't work. That you are valuable only if you do physical work.

T: So you're satisfied with your new activities?

K: Very. I can see that since I have dedicated more time to guitar playing, concerts, and painting, I feel completely different. I'm satisfied. I have regained the will to live. Before that, nothing I did made any sense to me, because I did everything just to please my mother. I didn't live for myself. I was appeasing her needs, not mine. And I'd like my mother to admit that what I do is alright.

Using self-judgment during the conversations, the client realizes again and again the devastating effect of external control on relationships. By understanding our behaviour as a whole, he also understands our physical and mental health. During the sessions, I presented to the client the concept of choice theory, he read Glasser's publications, but regardless of these new discoveries, he continued to return to his mother, to her behaviour, which he was still trying to change.

T: Your new activities turned out to be very good for you. If I understand you correctly, you want to have your mother's approval? What would this approval mean for you?

K: I just want her to say once in her life that I'm right.

T: Can you achieve that?

K: Maybe I could tell her more frequently so she'll understand.

T: But you have been trying that for years. Were you successful?

K: Not yet, but I won't give up like that.

T: I'm afraid that by trying to change your mother, you'll just end up harming yourself and not succeed in what you wish to achieve. I believe that we can't change others. I also don't see any problems with this kind of incomprehension, but in the fact that she behaves in a way that helps her appease her needs, and she doesn't want to hurt you. You said that your mother's aim is physical work and by bossing you around she ensures that, sadly this is a destructive way for you.

K: That's why I'd like her to consider me, her and others in the family to consider me.

T: Vid, now you are familiar with choice theory. Can you appease this need in another way? In a more effective way, in a way that will make you feel good?

K: I don't know. I'd like her to see that what I do is important, that it's work just as much.

T: You agree with the fact that you can't force your mother to behave as you want her to. You simply can't achieve that, otherwise you already would have. As you said, you've been trying for a long time.

K: I need an acknowledgement, that what I do is good.

T: You mean to say that only after that, would everything be really alright and good, when you mother says that?

K: That's right. Even though now it seems really ridiculous and unimportant.

T: You mentioned humiliation in the relationship with your mother. In this relationship, do you ever feel like equals?

K: Not at all. Near my mother I feel like a ten-year-old boy who needs instructions on what he can and can't do, what he has to do in order to make mum happy, without any right to his own opinion.

T: Maybe we could think of a way for you to feel more like an equal to her in the relationship.

K: Yes. I'd like to feel equal to her. But I don't know if it's even possible.

T: It's just about what you believe. About what you see and how you perceive yourself in the relationship with your mother. When would you feel equal to her?

K: I think when I took my own decisions.

T: Maybe you decide about something already?

K: Yes, where I go, what I wear, but not about what we need to do at home.

T: Maybe you could suggest what you can do at home?

K: I already suggested, for example, that we could play cards, since we frequently play, but others need to agree with that.

T: I understand.

K: But I feel like a child.

T: How do you behave in this situation? As an adult or a child?

K: More like a child, humbly and I get offended.

T: And how would an adult behave, how do you wish to feel?

K: I'd like to give my opinion, without feeling offended like a little child.

T: Could you do that?

K: I'd like to try. Until now I haven't even thought that I behave like a child. I just thought that it was my mother who treated me this way, that she was the one doing that.

This is an important insight for the client, by expressing his vision and explaining how others perceive and understand him, he was able to discover that solely he is responsible for his behaviour and that he can choose how to behave.

In the future, Vid's mother still tried to keep control over his behaviour with nagging and sarcastic remarks about "his art" or wasted time. However, at that moment Vid already knew that she was acting like this because she drew from her quality world (art is not as important to her as it is to Vid, she values working in the fields, around the house, etc. which are not as present in Vid's quality world as they are in hers) and that it does not mean that there is something wrong with him, and that what he does is important to him regardless of others' disapproval. The fact is that by playing guitar, reading what he wants, painting, and doing other activities, Vid began to live again. The words that Vid used to repeat: "I feel great", "I'm very satisfied", "full of energy", "I'm thinking differently", "I started to love life again", etc., told me that he was successfully appeasing his psychic needs, because those activities helped him connect with others.

In that period, Vid established a connection with a friend from the past. In truth, she has been in love with him, but Vid rejected her and now he sees in her the woman with whom he would like to spend the rest of his life. They both like music, he showed her support in what she does —she sings in a choir and he goes to her performances. She frequently invites him to her place for dinner, they both like good food, they like to read and talk about what they read, they listen to classical music, laugh together, she translates texts for him, etc. With her, he feels relaxed and accepted. They talk about life together, but they have realized that even if their friendship means a lot to both of them, so does freedom, that's why they both prefer to meet occasionally instead of starting a life together. The planning of a family also presented some problems since they are both older; she is forty-five and has numerous limitations for getting pregnant. Besides that, Vid realizes that now he has a lot of free time and a family would bring duties, responsibilities, which he somewhat fears, but most of all he does not know how he would provide for his family financially. He retired early due to his ill health and receives a low pension. She teaches foreign languages in a high school and she is economically independent, used to a comfortable lifestyle, as Vid said. Since they both know what they want in life or what is good for them, they postponed the decision of a life together until a future time, so they could spend some time together and see how their relationship evolves. During my sessions with Vid, he was very satisfied with the relationship; he especially stressed that she accepts him as he is, which is of course very important.

Despite this relationship, Vid conserves his independency and freedom, he frequently goes alone for a Sunday trip, takes a walk along the River Soča, and goes to parties at a friend's place. Vid's relationship with his friends was very important during the process of his "healing". They invited him to go out with them, to go on picnics during the summer; they encouraged him, but the most important fact for him was that they did not ask him about his "illness", they accepted him, had fun together, supported him, and respected his talents.

In the period during which he was coming to therapy, Vid thought a lot, searched for solutions, more efficient behaviours, and wrote down some reflections on our sessions. He started reading the publications of Trstenjak on his own and, and on my recommendation, also Glasser.

A confirmation that Vid is now successfully appeasing his needs is the fact that he does not see himself as a sick person, because he believes that he is the one controlling his life. He realizes that he is the one creating his present happiness. He emphasizes discipline, planning his day, activities, etc. These things proved very effective for him. He is conscious about the meaning of satisfying relationships, because he has experienced good and less good relationships and he also connects them with his problems. He acts more in line with his quality world, and he tries to understand his mother, who grew up without a father and had to work in order to survive. She brought up her children in the spirit of hard work and tried to teach them the notions, so that they would know how to work, since working means surviving.

It also seems important to mention that Vid reduced his smoking, which I'm linking to the fact that he found a better way to appease his needs. In the morning, he exercises regularly and takes walks. He works for himself, his health, and his happiness.

Vid says that he suffered for forty years, that he does not want to blame anyone for his unhappiness; he now can recognize his mother's behaviours – her exerting control, giving orders, underestimating him, insulting, and criticizing him. Since I believed that he was exposed to his mother's external control psychology, I assumed that he also adopted some parts of this behaviour.

Further on, I will present a part of the session regarding the client's use of external control psychology in the relationship with his brother, the client's realization about his actions, and our search for possible solutions for a different behaviour.

T: Vid, you mentioned your younger brother with whom you live now. How would you describe your relationship, are you perhaps allies in the relationship with your mother?

K: (laughs) We're allies in the relationship with our mother to a point. She persecutes us both, but we also use each other as an excuse. As an older brother, I believe that I have more rights and I believe that he should listen to me.

T: What does this mean, that he should listen to you?

K: That he should do what I tell him to.

T: For example?

K: I don't know, let's say I tell him to bring the wood, I then expect him to do that.

T: And when he doesn't?

K: I get angry and I let him know that he should obey me.

T: You mean that he should obey you as you obey your mother?

K: Yes, like that.

T: What does this mean to you, that he obeys you?

K: That he knows who to respect!

T: Do you respect your mother because she gives you orders? I mean, do you respect her more because she gives you orders?

K: Respect her?! I know I respect her, but I don't know if it's because she gives me orders. When she does, she makes me nervous, she annoys me, at that moment I don't respect her.

T: What do you feel then?

K: I feel anger and also a little hatred, because she doesn't leave me alone.

T: So how can you expect your brother to feel differently towards you when you give him orders?

K: Because I want him to respect me.

T: Have you ever thought to gain his respect in some other way?

K: I don't know; I've never thought of that.

T: You said you don't respect your mother because she is bossy and insults you. I'd like to know which of her characteristics make you respect her.

K: She's a hardworking woman, she's attentive, she cooks for me and my brother, washes our clothes, irons them, she taught us a lot of practical things, and now that I think of it, she constantly teaches us new ones.

T: Good, now I know that your mother also has a lot of good qualities.

K: She certainly has her qualities, I admit to that.

T: You mean that you tell her so?

K: Yes, I tell her and I can see that she likes when I admit it.

T: I believe you, we all want others to see and accept what we do. That's why I think it is important that we tell each other, as you said, that we acknowledge others' qualities. What do you think are the qualities that your brother values in you?

K: He often says that I'm intelligent, that I remember a lot, that I have the will to read for hours, because he can't, he doesn't have enough concentration. He also tells me that I'm stubborn.

T: Do you take that as a compliment?

K: Yes, for me it is a compliment, because of my stubbornness I can achieve may things, like discipline, perseverance.

T: So, you mentioned some characteristics that could help get another person's respect. Can you say that your brother respects you for everything you just said?

K: I think he does. At least he should.

T: Do you still believe that you could get others' respect by giving orders, delegating?

K: I don't believe we can gain respect that way, but I still believe that he should obey me.

The client still believes that he can appease his need for power with the use of external control psychology; for this reason I will pass to the client's relationship with his brother with the intention of making the client judge the influence of his behaviour on their relationship, so we can try to find new, more appropriate behaviours in their relationship.

T: Yes, we talked about obeying. Let's return to the relationship with your brother. You said that your relationship is not the best. Do you want a better relationship with him?

K: Of course I'd like to be a better friend to him, but we're too different.

T: It's true that we're all different, but it's also true that we live together and that it's better for us to accept one another if we want to understand each other and get along.

K: Yes, but he underestimates me and that angers me. Why does he have to get mixed up with art if he doesn't have a clue about it?

T: That's your brother's behaviour. What's yours?

K: I tell him what he needs to hear, the brat. He has never done anything in his life that has some worth or weight: he's not going to judge my work, my pictures!

T: Are you getting closer to your brother with that behaviour? Do you believe that you'll get closer if you continue to think about him like this?

K: No, it's not bringing us closer, normally it all ends with a fight.

T: What does bring you closer? When do you feel the closest to your brother?

K: To tell the truth, there's not much that bring us closer. We're very different people.

T: Maybe we can now think about bringing you closer to your brother? Do you agree?

K: We could do that together.

T: During our meetings you managed to change the relationship with your mother. Even if we found out that your quality worlds differ quite a bit, you found a way to get closer to her. Could we first resume the behaviours you used to connect with your mother?

K: Yes. Since I know that work means a lot to her, I ask her frequently if I can help her with something, I also offer to make lunch. She's a very good cook so sometimes she shows me some tricks and I'm happy to learn something new. I often go to the supermarket; I never did that before. I think it's important that I often tried to make her read something, because I really wanted her to, and now that I don't force her anymore, she frequently takes a book and reads it. After that we talk as I always wanted. That makes me happy.

The client chose the behaviours that help both him and his mother appease their need for power. Since he and his brother both want to be the important one, I thought that we should choose the behaviours that would help them both realize their sense of importance, power, and value and connect them and bring them closer at the same time. I followed the client's suggestions and the selection of new behaviours.

T: Vid, what you listed is excellent. I believe that now you feel better in your mother's company.

K: It's true. Now I like spending time with her, before I was more afraid of her than happy.

T: Could you use some of the tested behaviours in your relationship with your brother?

K: It would be difficult.

T: What if we start with his quality world? What's the most important thing to him?

K: Since he stopped drinking, he cycles a lot. It doesn't interest me, but I think it would be good for my health if I started to exercise a bit.

T: Do you mean that you'd go cycling with your brother?

K: Yes, I would, I know that it would make him very happy.

T: It would make him happy, but what would it do for you? You said that exercise would be good for your health. Would you gain anything else by going cycling with him?

K: We'd spend some time together, I believe that we wouldn't be fighting, we'd enjoy the nature, which I love. Maybe we would have time to talk, since it's difficult to do that at home. It would also depend on where we went, but I think I'd have something to say about what we'd see.

T: Aha, you found some interesting possibilities. Do you think that you should take notice of anything in particular, so that your cycling would be successful?

K: I think that I should let him lead me, I shouldn't get involved in what he suggests.

T: Could you do that?

K: I think I could, because some other time it would be my turn (laugh).

T: Would a chance like that, for cycling I mean, present itself soon?

K: My brother cycles every day, so I could join him tomorrow afternoon.

T: Perfect. Next time we could talk about your activity together.

The relationship between me and the client helped him appease his need for power (you know that well, you have many qualities, you succeeded, you knew, etc.) and helped him to learn how to let himself and others successfully appease their need for power and also other needs.

At the present time, Vid is satisfied with the relationships at home. He believes they all get along better, they are more relaxed, they joke more, and most of their fighting revolves around politics. I believe they will have to struggle every day to reach a mutual understanding and that old habits will eventually die out.

Further on during our sessions, the client became aware of some other behaviours. Above all, he is especially proud of having improved the relationships with their neighbours, with whom his parents have had quarrels over the years. At first, he thought about, as he said, humiliating himself and making the first step. Then he realized that he was doing it for himself, because these quarrels have been bothering him for years and he wanted better relationships with his neighbours. After years of silence, Vid started talking with his neighbour and after some time he invited him for a coffee. He said that his behaviour helped him get to know an interesting person. They were both very satisfied with this meeting. They found out that they are both interested in history and so they met more often. Vid's parents still don't talk with the neighbours, but Vid sees himself as a free being, who can have relationships with anyone, regardless of others' desires, and that way he can successfully appease his needs.

The client started to see himself as an important person, he started to take into consideration his desires and needs and by doing that he realized that he is the main agent in their realization.

I am sure that Vid has a strong control over his life, since he clearly says that he does not think of himself as an ill person and that he has never felt so happy and fulfilled in his life. He wants to continue doing the activities that make him happy and he plans to gain new knowledge in the future. He is very interested in psychology.

Psychosomatic problems (couples therapy)

We talk about a psychosomatic illness when we are referring to a painful emotional behaviour (headaches and back pains are among the most typical) where no structural changes to tissue or organs occur. Partner therapy, which addresses the health problems of both spouses, exposes the connection between a bad condition and a bad relationship. As it will be possible to see from the presented extracts of the present therapeutic conversation, their relationship is based mainly on control, criticism, reproaches, blame, power measurements, failed attempts to exert control, and gaining attention, acceptance, and consideration. For many years now, they have been living in a vicious circle, full of controlling behaviours and thus losing – each in their own way – control over their own lives and their marriage.

Before treating their problems, both clients gave assurance that no medical research showed any organic cause for their problems.

Ana and Ivo are an older married couple who have been living for many years in an unsatisfying, even painful relationship. Their marriage does not reflect the traditional values – to be considered, respected, appreciated and, of course, loved. The couple live in a marriage that differs immensely from the traditional idea of marriage. Their creative system tries to find a way to restore control in their marriage, but these attempts throughout the years have been unsuccessful. That is why they opted for therapy.

Ana talked about her creative thoughts – what was she prepared to do to have her husband all to herself or to be more appreciated and respected than her biggest opponent, her husband's mother. Through her frustrations, she tries to deal with ordinary emotional behaviours, like complaining and being angry, and she is slowly turning her dissatisfaction into depression.

Their resistance against trying to exert control over one another and their unsuccessful attempts to control themselves present themselves in a hurtful way, and also with pain. Ana suffers from severe and frequent headaches and Ivo has a drinking and some somatic problems (he complained a lot of lower back pain). Both spouses are overweight.

Ivo's drinking is a typical attempt to feel like he has escaped the control that is exerted over him at home, but this intoxication is just making him lose control over his own life.

Part of the first conversation – it was intended to establish a connection, a safe therapist-client relationship, to become familiar with the problems and thus interpret them, to identify the behaviours in their relationship, and for my interpretation of what I saw and heard – is already giving some insights and the gaining of new beliefs for both clients.

T: You say it's time to change your life. What are you thinking about?

I: We realized that we cannot continue this way. We are not getting any younger and our life is getting too difficult. I think that we cannot continue like this, something has to be done.

T: Can you describe what you have in mind when you say that your life is too difficult? What do you mean by saying that you cannot go on like this?

I: I cannot talk normally with her anymore. Whatever I say is wrong. She starts rolling her eyes, or she swings her arm and she tells me to go somewhere, or she replies curtly. And then the fighting starts, because I can't stand the way she talks to me. I'd like to talk to her, but it's impossible.

A: You don't want to talk, you want to give orders, so that everything would be as you say. And if I don't agree, there's a fight coming.

I: Then why do you just turn your back and leave? You don't talk!

A: Because you're getting on my nerves, I can't stand you and your mother anymore. From the moment that I set foot into the household, it's was than thirty years ago, there was never a steak on my plate, like I'm not part of your family. You know (she turns to me), I've had it, I'm worn down. I can't do this anymore.

T: I believe that during the years there's a lot of unpleasantness that accumulates itself in a marriage and because of that we are unhappy and we don't feel good in such a marriage. You two have already came to the conclusion that you don't want a marriage like that. I'd like to know what expectations and hopes for your marriage bring you here. Do you want to preserve your marriage and work on it in order to improve it, or are you thinking about divorce? What do you want? What are your thoughts on the subject? Ana?

A: I'm not thinking about separation, although it's hard, I won't say it isn't. We've had crises all the time and we survived them. A separation or a divorce is not an option, where would I go, I don't have anything that's mine and I have just enough money to survive. But in spite of all that, I don't want to end the marriage.

T: So, it means that you're prepared to invest in your marriage, to contribute to its improvement?

A: Yes, even if I don't exactly know what it means to work on it.

At first I thought it was a too early for a professional point of view, for explaining choice theory, especially because I hadn't checked yet whether the other spouse wanted help too. I could only assume that they had come with a common goal. Despite the hesitations, I thought it was a good opportunity for me to talk about the possibility of choosing behaviours – behaviours that build and strengthen a relationship, and behaviours that are "deadly" for a marriage. I referred to what Ana had said earlier and started encouraging.

T: It's good that you said you are going to work on it. I believe that each one of us can choose and control his own behaviour, but not the behaviour of others. And that the behaviours we choose are very important for our relationships. By choosing behaviours like insulting, reproaching, extorting, threatening and others, we contribute to the destruction of a relationship, or in this case a marriage. But on the other hand, with behaviours like listening, supporting, considering, respecting, and accepting, we strengthen and consolidate the relationship. If your goal is to save the marriage, then it would be proper to use the kind of behaviours that improve and strengthen it.

A: I understand, but I don't know if this can be applied when he comes home drunk and he despises me and insults me. How can I respect him then?

T: With difficulty. Maybe it would be better if, for a start, you realized that you can control only your behaviour and not your husband's too.

A: I know that, because no matter what I do, he always does things his own way.

T: Good. I suggest we stop there a for a moment. I'd like to ask you too, Sir, what do you want regarding your marriage?

I: I thought I wouldn't get my turn today, that she'd do all the talking as always.

I deliberately ignored his reproaches, wanting to show him that he cannot control me with those kinds of pressuring attempts. I calmly repeated the question.

T: Do you want help for your marriage?

I: Of course, I do, that's why I'm here. We don't need help from others to pack our things and go our separate ways.

T: Good. What do you think about the idea that you can control only your own behaviour?

I: To control my own behaviour? Does this mean I cannot make her obey me?

T: Yes, that's what it means.

I: That's not true. I can make her obey me.

T: But she alone decides whether she'll obey you. In that moment, it's a better decision than not obeying, especially if there are threats involved. But your wife can choose differently. She chooses her own behaviours, you cannot choose them for her. Can I make you do something that you don't want to?

I: No, you can't, that's not possible.

T: That's correct. And you too can't control my behaviour. That is choice theory. It asserts that the only behaviour that we can control is our own.

A: Then why do I have to do everything that he tells me?

T: Do you really have to? Do you really do everything that your husband tells you to?

A: No, not everything, but most of it.

T: But ultimately you are the one who decides whether to do it or not.

A: I've never thought about it this way. It seemed to me that I have to, that it's not my decision.

T: Yes, these kinds of realizations give you the feeling of getting control back over your own life, that in fact we are the ones who choose and reach a decision. But we opt for what seems better at the moment. Our behaviour has always a purpose, we want to attain something with it, maybe even for someone to leave us alone.

I: I can agree with that. She provokes me, but when I say something, when I show who the master of the house is, it all goes wrong.

T: We said that we can control our own behaviour; this means that my behaviour doesn't depend on someone else's behaviour. Therefore, I don't need to behave like someone else does, or as someone else expects. I can decide otherwise. I have that possibility. And becoming angry is a behaviour and thus I can decide not to choose it.

I: Yes, maybe, I think that's very difficult. We were taught this way.

T: I agree, in time our behaviours can become part of our habits. At least the ones with which it seems like we're gaining something, but in reality, they're harmful. We'll talk more about this later. We have to abandon this kind of behaviours or replace them with new, more effective ones in order to feel better.

A: Yes, I'd like to feel better again.

T: Could you pay attention to the kind of behaviours that you choose until our meeting next week? Would you try to choose more behaviours that bring you closer, establish a more solid connection between the two of you, so that you can feel better in your marriage?

A: So, I'll take care of my own behaviour?

T: Yes. That's exactly what it means. And you, Ivo, try to take care of your own behaviour, use those that will get you closer to your goal – to feel good in your marriage.

I: I agree. Everyone takes care of his own behaviour.

T: This means that you won't reproach, threaten or insult one another, that you'll be attentive, take each other into consideration, listen to each other, try to be well disposed to one another. Is that acceptable for you?

A: We'll try and we'll see how it goes.

In my first conversation with the clients my goal was not to take sides, neither his nor hers, but I have to take the side of their marriage. That is why they came to me. I was very attentive to that, because I was aware of the fact that otherwise I might "lose" one of them, and that would impact our further work and their marriage. This is why I was constantly using the word marriage, so they would realize that we are talking about a thing common to both of them, and that it would be the focus of our future work.

Maybe the agreement regarding their behaviour until next meeting is a little too general; at this moment they certainly do not know what exactly this means for them, in their everyday life. I think that it's important for them first to become aware that they choosing their behaviours and to gain the feeling of deciding (for themselves, not for the other one), so in the future we will be able to discuss some activities that they could do together for the sake of their marriage.

In our next session, I first focused on their choices regarding their behaviour in the past week, during which we had not seen each other. As expected, it turns out that the stimulus-response psychology is deeply rooted in their subconscious and that it is not possible to get rid of it in such a short period of time, therefore I will repeatedly talk about it and try to explain it, estimate it, and try to make them aware of it in order to make them really believe that they choose whether to act this way or not and so that choice theory becomes their new belief.

Further on, I wanted to know what they still define as good in their marriage. I'm researching their sources, what can we work on, and where can we find some possibilities for new and better choices.

T: Can you both, please, try to think about what are the good parts of your marriage? What are you satisfied with in your marriage?

I: I don't know what's good, but I know there's lot of bad. The constant arguing, quarrels, she doesn't even want to eat with me anymore, let alone anything else.

A: Why should I eat with you when you don't even see me?! You eat with your mother. I, as your wife, don't even exist in that house. Your mother is the important one, not me!

I: It's not true, you know it's not true! Where should I put her? She's my mom.

A: And I'm your wife, but you are not as attentive to me as you are to her. You don't care about me. And she acts like you're hers.

I: You just think that. I do take care of you. What else am I doing? I take care of both of you, and the children too.

T: If I may intervene … This, what you were talking about now, is what is bad in your marriage. Let's look together at what's good. Could we say, Ana, that Ivo is an attentive husband, father and also son?

A: Yes, I can say that he's attentive. He worries a lot when things look bad for us and there's not enough money. He does his best, he often works alone with meat and then he sells salami and sausages so it is easier for us.

T: Does this give you a feeling of safety?

A: Yes, it does. I know that without him it would be a lot worse, I don't even know how it would be.

T: What else do you appreciate about Ivo?

A: I feel that he's not a womanizer, I'm not scared of that. He also doesn't criticise me because of my looks. I'm weak-eyed, these thick glasses, and also my years are showing in other ways. I don't remember him ever letting me know that.

I: To me she's still beautiful and I still want her.

T: What you said is very beautiful. Can you tell this to her, to your wife?

I: Of course. Ana, to me you're still the most beautiful woman and you know I miss us sleeping together.

A: I have no interest in that anymore.

I: But I do. You didn't even hear that you're beautiful to me.

A: I did, what you said is beautiful, but in reality, I don't feel that way, your behaviour towards me doesn't make me feel that way. There are too many ugly words.

T: And now you have the chance to tell each other what you respect, admire about the other. Ana?

A: I don't know, he's hardworking, I can say that he does a lot of work around the house. He and his mother reproach me with laziness and I don't know what more can I do! Like everything I do is not enough.

T: Let's stick with the good. Ivo?

I: Ana is an attentive housewife and a good cook. I have never complained about that. But this Sunday I made an effort and made roast meat and potatoes, and when I wanted the three of us to sit at the table, she started grumbling about the mess I had made in the kitchen, the way I had prepared the meal … Just because I didn't make it her way. She spoiled everything, I got mad and left.

A: To the bar. To play cards and drink.

I: Yes, to the bar, where I can relax.

T: We all feel better where we are accepted, popular, where no one tries to control us. And friends at the bar offer us just that. But we remain unhappy, unsatisfied in our relationships with other people. You told each other some good qualities, that could maybe help you moving forward. How could you satisfy your need for understanding, acceptance in your relationship?

A: I have started to think that he feels much better in the bar with his friends. That's why he spends there so much time there and why he goes there so often. I have never understood what the hell he gets there!

I: It's exactly how you said. No one bothers me there.

A: Are you saying that I bother you?

I: That's how I feel. I'll be honest. When I'm home I feel like being on a rack, on one side it's you pulling me and on the other it's my mother, and I just want to please you both.

A: Now I just realized that I have never asked you how you feel. All this time I've been concerned just about my dissatisfaction.

I: I think all three of us are unhappy. I feel like I should promise now that I'll never behave like I have until now.

T: It would be good for your relationship to abandon these behaviours. Besides, you don't need to promise anything to anyone, just to yourself.

I: I think we should continue from where it turned bad the last time – from choosing these other, better behaviours. What do you say, Ana?

A: We didn't do very well last time. I agree that we should try again.

T: All right. Maybe this week you can make another step and try to choose behaviours that could bring you closer, maybe you could use some behaviours from the past that turned out to be good for you. By doing this you can pay attention to your feelings, how you feel when choosing these new behaviours.

This text is, above of all, a display of a wide range of behaviours harmful for a marriage and for the individuals in it. A lot of reproaches, expressed several times (in order to be heard, taken into consideration), a lot of resentment, reciprocal blame, laying guilt, etc. In short, there is a lot of helplessness and unhappiness hidden in all these hurting behaviours, for which the couple (still) believe that these behaviours will help them change one another, that the other will realize what they are doing wrong and how to do it right.

Without a doubt, Ana thinks she's the victim. Her posture and her words express her belief that she's being wronged, that she is a powerless victim, and that others run her life. In her relationship with her husband and his mother she does not feel accepted, loved, important, etc., or in the language of choice theory: she does not appease her basic psychic needs in her relationships with close relatives. That is why she started to develop auto destructive behaviours soon after they started living together. It was an attempt to appease her needs, trying to change the behaviours of other people. Of course, she could not succeed because it is impossible to change the behaviour of someone else. She did not develop her behaviours and her beliefs in her relationships with new people, that is why she is unhappy today, and her unhappiness manifests itself in various ways, as far as with mental health problems and pain.

Ivo took the position of the stronger one in their relationship. He has his wife and mother fussing around him, which gives him a feeling of power, importance, and worth. At the same time, it is possible to identify feelings like entrapment, powerlessness, because one side (the wife or the mother) always remains dissatisfied. Whatever he does, he cannot take both of them into consideration (they are on two different sides). Moreover, he feels unsuccessful, because in reality he cannot manage to realize in the best possible way his belief that, as the only man in the family, he has to provide for their financial security. I think these are his distresses and he expresses them through male forms of dissatisfaction, i.e. alcohol abuse and pain that is acceptable for men (back, lower back pains) and through that he tries to assure himself power and control.

I think it was important and also necessary to clearly tell the couple what our main goal is –their marriage. We are not working on only one of them. Even if this time they have also tried to win me over to "his or her" side, I persistently sided with their marriage. It seemed the only reasonable decision.

It would bode well for both spouses and their marriage to experience the effectiveness of new behaviours, otherwise they will hang onto their old beliefs about the effectiveness of external control psychology. It does not help that there are two of them and that the alliance they have formed, even if it is "rotten", represents a risk that they will strongly cling onto old beliefs and persist in using destructive behaviours. If one or both of them preserve the external control psychology, there is a great possibility that their marriage will fail or that they will continue to live unhappily in it.

Further on, I plan to explain to the clients the concept of holistic behaviour and to show them the connection between their health problems and their chosen behaviours and beliefs. But before that, I'm interested in their quality world, what are the images through which they try to appease their psychic needs. I foresee that it will be necessary to create new images that will replace the existing ones, which have or will prove themselves as unattainable, or maybe it will be necessary to create completely new images that will help them appease their needs more successfully. I'm also interested in the most important image in their quality world – their self-image.

T: You say that since you started using fewer forcing behaviours, you have fewer conflicts. I think that today we should take a look at the activities that make you both happy and maybe those you haven't done in a long time or haven't even tried yet. What do you think?

A: I have a lot of desires but there's no money to realize them. And maybe I'll never be able to.

T: Can you tell me more about your desires?

A: Since I was young, I've dreamed about what other parts of the world look like, how people live elsewhere. But in reality, I've never been anywhere, there's only work at home. He has never wanted to hear about what I want. I could only take care of the family and work. That yes, but having fun no, God no!

I: We have very different desires, you know. I enjoy working, but everything is difficult for her.

T: I suggest you focus on yourself. What is it that makes you happy? What do you want to do?

I: I like to stay home, I don't mind not going anywhere. Maybe, when the children were little, I wanted to travel, but I dedicated all my time to building the house. In that period, I didn't have time to fish either, so I gave it up. Sometimes I still think about it, I think that walking by the river and fishing calmed me, I felt a special peace, I was alone with myself, I remember the serenity that I felt.

T: Do you miss those feelings?

I: Yes, I miss them. I'm very nervous and I think that I can calm down only when I drink.

T: I invite you to think together about the things that you have in common. We believe that the children moving away from home often shows the holes that have formed in a marriage. But the time when children move out is also a chance for the spouses to "come first" once again and to dedicate themselves to each other.

I: I think that's what happened in our case. Ana has now become more annoying and unsatisfied because she can't turn her attention to our daughter and son so much.

T: Do you too feel the need for common activities?

I: Yes, I'd like to get close again. Our relationship has lots of holes, but I think that things have calmed down a little, for one there's less fighting.

T: What are you thinking about, any ideas about where you see the two of you together?

A: So, as I know us, I'd say that we enjoyed ourselves by watching movies. I don't remember when the last time was that we watched a good movie; now we follow politics and social themes. In the past I liked to have fun, I was relaxed, but I haven't seen myself like that in a long time.

I: I think it's a good idea. I'd be very happy to watch a movie.

T: You can watch a movie together, but I don't know how much would that help your relationship. We are talking about what's good for your marriage. So, it would be better to find something that connects you, something personal. What do you say?

A: It's difficult to say what that would be. I think it's impossible to go anywhere, I don't know who would take care of his mother.

I: Barbara (their oldest daughter) can visit and take care of her, that shouldn't be a problem. The only question is where we would go. We cannot afford anything expensive at the moment.

T: Perhaps you would enjoy some time alone. When was the last time you were alone?

A: I don't remember, I really don't. His mother was always there, which drives me to even bigger despair.

I: Just now, I was thinking about our farm; what if we go up there to take a look? I think that it is really peaceful there and right now everything is green. I wish I were up there right now.

A: And what will we be doing there? We'll work again. I'll cook and clean and you'll work around the house. Like when I'm home.

I: It wouldn't be like at home. And we don't need to work. I don't have that intention. We can enjoy the nature. We could go for a walk, down to the stream, you could pick snowdrops, we could lounge, talk. What do you say?

A: It's okay with me as long as we don't work. But I can really picture you taking walks and picking flowers (laughs). Can we stay longer?

I: If I say I won't work, then I won't work. I will take walks, but you'll be the one picking flowers (laughs). We can stay from Friday to Sunday.

A: You mean this weekend?

I: Yes, it's going to be really nice, weather wise.

A: Agreed, we're going.

T: Nicely done. I think it's important that in these three days you don't say or do anything that you know would destroy the good climate in your relationship and that would divide you. I wish you a nice weekend.

These kinds of conciliatory discussions between spouses are a good sign for their marriage. They try to come to an agreement, to compromise, say things that will not cause anger, and accept (with humour) their characteristics. With that, the clients showed a real interest and willingness to save their marriage and that, despite everything, they both have enough optimism to continue. I think they reached a point where they really realize that it's up to them to change things and to make it all better, otherwise they risk increasing their unhappiness and completely destroying the marriage.

The purpose of common activities is to feel connected once again, to see each other in a different light, outside of everyday life, which they could not handle for some time. And what is more important, they are alone. So, the wife doesn't not feel like she comes second in the competition for her husband's attention and he does not feel like he's on a rack between one and the other constraint. There is a possibility that they will awaken old feelings, remember an old, good quality, but more importantly they will realize that they can still enjoy things – together and even after all these years.

Of course, we should not expect that these three days, as beautiful as they can be, can do miracles for their marriage. But it will certainly be a good start in the process of improving their relationship. In their feedback, they said that it was "nothing special", but that they hadn't had such a nice time in years. They confessed to each other that they tried to enjoy as much as possible the time spent together and that they did not "come to any disagreements". It is also very encouraging for their marriage that after several years they have been intimate again.

I think it's important to "revive" the images from their quality world, in the sense of what kind of a person I want to be, what makes me happy, what brings me joy, what do I need and how, or in which way I used to realize that. I understand the "revival" of the images in the quality world as an awakening of a person, because our thinking and our activities are in accordance with the images created, so our "personal album" is the source of our new choices. That is why I think that in the process of changing our beliefs and choosing new behaviours it's important for each person to become aware of the "images" in his "personal album", because that is how he can recognize his desires and needs, but also the ways of how to reach and appease them.

Further on, I'm going to present the discussion in which I introduced to the couple Glasser's "marriage circle" or the "rescue circle".

T: You must have noticed that from the beginning I've been talking about your marriage. We're talking about what's good for your marriage, how to preserve it, improve it, all this time we've been working on your marriage and for it. In your experience, you sometimes still use the old controlling behaviours and you still encounter some problems. It's important that in these moments you know how to act for the good of your marriage. In that case, you can rely on the solution circle, which you enter once you realize that you're using destructive behaviours with which you try to control or change the other's behaviour. In that case, you can discuss what can each of you do – by taking into consideration the knowledge that you can control only your own behaviour –in order to solve the problem.

I: This means that I invite Ana to step into the circle if I start getting angry, because of something that isn't the way I want it? And then we talk?

T: Yes, in this circle you don't use destructive behaviours, not even anger, but other behaviours that are good for your marriage, for example listening, supporting, connecting, discussing, and other behaviours that will bring you closer.

A: What if neither of us mentions the circle, if we continue to argue?

T: You are the ones who decide that. When you have your marriage before your eyes and the realization that everything you do has to be for its good, I believe that you won't even have to use the circle that often, because you'll be solving your disagreements before that. But if you stick to your convictions, to what is important to each of you, you'll find yourselves on your old path and your marriage will find itself in a bad place again.

A: Just like everything really depends only on us.

T: I believe that it actually depends on you. No one can have as much influence on your marriage as the two of you. As we established before, no one can make you unhappy unless you see and feel that way. There are no reactions to the stimuli, there are just choices.

A: I know, but I'm afraid that I'll start yelling and insulting him again when he comes home drunk. His drinking makes me angry. I mean, I get angry. What can I do in the circle with him if he's drunk?

T: What does all this yelling at him about him being drunk bring you?

A: What does it bring me? It brings me nothing, I just get really angry.

T: I believe that it brings you something, otherwise you wouldn't yell at him and insult him. Does it perhaps give you a feeling of power, supremacy, and control over him?

A: And what can I do with that power if the next day I'm the one who's subjected to him again? He's the householder.

At this point, there was clearly presented an unsatisfied need for power, control, and being heard in the relationship with her husband. I thought it was important to focus on it.

T: Can you obtain this power in some other way? You realized that the one you have when your husband is drunk doesn't last long. Can you find some other way to regularly appease this need?

A: I'd like to have the final word at least regarding the housekeeping. I think that lately he wants to take the lead on that too.

T: What does it mean to you to have the final word regarding the housekeeping, as you say?

A: That I'm the one who knows more about it.

I: But I do admit that you're more familiar with the housekeeping. When I do something little it's just to show you that I can do something too and that you don't need to spend all your time in the kitchen, it's not because you're not a good cook. It's far from that.

T: Can you see your husband's "involving" himself in the household chores in that way?

A: I can, I never thought that he had good intentions. I thought that he wanted to teach me so I'd see how to do things right.

T: If we go back to the question about the behaviour you choose when your husband comes home drunk. Do you believe that you'll prevent him from getting drunk again by attacking and insulting him?

A: No, I don't believe that anymore. Otherwise he'd have already stopped, considering that I've been attacking him because of that since we've been together.

T: Now you know why you haven't had any success, because it's not in your power to change his behaviour. But you can change yours. Or do the attacks and insults contribute to the improvement of your marriage?

A: Of course not. What should I do then?

T: What should you do? What kind of possibilities do you see?

A: I can turn around and continue to sleep.

T: What would you achieve with that?

A: I wouldn't get upset and there would be no fighting.

T: So, this is a better choice that the former one.

A: Yes, it's better. But I'd still want to talk to him in the morning when he sobers up.

T: That would be reasonable. But without the insulting, criticizing, reproaching …

A: I'll try not to use all that, and if I'm not able to do it, I'll use the circle.

T: What do you think about your wife's thoughts, Ivo?

I: I think it's almost impossible that there would be no yelling and attacking when I come home. I'll be very surprised if everything is as she just said. I think I'll be coming home earlier than usual, because now I know what to expect, so it doesn't matter to me when I come home, I'm yelled at anyway. We'll see.

Further on, I steered the conversation towards the importance of a good relationship – a successful satisfying of the needs in their relationship by preventing the use of behaviours that give a person a false feeling of control over his life.

For Ana and Ivo, the rescue circle or the marriage circle represented a lifeline in situations where they couldn't abandon compulsory actions. Especially in recurrent frustrations, they frequently held on to old behaviours and after some time they managed to make new choices, which is very positive for their marriage.

The clients thought about the connection between their mutual (lack of) understanding and their health problems. At one of our therapeutic sessions, they stressed their understanding of holistic behaviour and the explanation that a psychosomatic illness represents the destruction of our creative system. On that occasion, they performed a self-estimation regarding their new choices, the change of the adopted beliefs, and their health problems (physical and mental ones).

A: I remember you saying once that we are the ones that create the bad feelings and health problems.

T: In a way, yes. It happens as a result of our best attempts to obtain what we desire, to realize the images we have of ourselves or of others, that are preserved in our quality world. That's why we talk about headaches, pains, depression – by using these, Glasser reminds us that it's our choice. And that give us the feeling of control. What's your experience?

A: It's difficult to get used to it, because we always used to say that we had a headache. I noticed that my head hurts when I'm upset and angry. Now I understand why. And I have a hard time understanding, as you say, what the thing that I get with these headaches is.

T: We discussed that our behaviour is holistic, that by choosing what we do and think, we indirectly influence our feelings and physiology, the activity of our organism. Based on this kind of understanding of human behaviour, we talked about new choices, therefore about new activities and the change of beliefs – our consideration of something. That's only logical. When people are in distress, we focus on the symptomatology, because that's what we feel, it's more noticeable. Let's say our heart is beating faster, our hands shake, we sweat, we feel a knot in our stomach, in the throat, we blush, etc. That depends on what our "talents" are. I just want to tell you that occupying ourselves with physical signs and also with feelings doesn't help us to feel better. These are just signals that we're not feeling well at the moment and that it's time to do a self-estimation – about what we think and do.

A: This explanation helps me a lot and it's very logical. We have also talked a lot about choices. But I don't understand the fact that we choose pain.

T: In accordance with choice theory, we understand the psychosomatic illness as an indirect creative choice. If we constantly use something, it tells us that it brings us something that we gain from it. Often, the illness can give us a certain amount of control over others, with the purpose of satisfying our needs. It's typical for people who suffer from a psychosomatic illness that they keep inside them their anger, resentment, a controlling emotional behaviour that for some unknown reason they don't show, because it may not be in accordance with the beliefs they have adopted. One of these labels is: "boys don't cry" or "if you get angry, you're ugly".

A: I was always told that as a woman, I have to endure. But a man doesn't have to?!

T: Probably not. Eve was conceived from Adam's rib and after that the poor woman offered him an apple (laugh). I'm saying that numerous stereotypes originate from Christian traditions and they are embedded in our thinking, our beliefs, they are the filter of our perception and our activities are in accordance with our beliefs.

I: What we decide to do and how do we decide to act is very important. When I think about that I don't know what's right anymore. Is it better to get angry or to repress the anger?

T: By getting angry we just try to control someone else, to make him do what we want. It's not that we repress our anger, it's about looking at other people's behaviour in another way, so we don't get angry by thinking or looking at that and we find other ways to appease our needs more successfully in our relationship towards this person. By improving our relationships and appeasing our physical needs, we don't need destructive creativity. And that is the purpose of therapy – to regain control over your life with new and better choices.

In the therapeutic process, I haven't paid any attention, at least not directly, to the symptomatology (pains, overeating, alcohol abuse, etc.). Because in accordance with choice theory I presumed that the presented symptoms are caused by an important unsatisfying relationship (the two spouses came to therapy with the same self-evaluation in mind). This means that the spouses do not appease their basic physical needs in their relationship, at least not successfully. They are victims of the external control psychology and maybe both, or at least one of them, use it.

I always followed this conviction as the spouses started describing the symptoms, complaining about their physical problems. Through questions, thinking, and acting, I "positioned" them on the "front wheels" of their holistic behaviour. It seemed that neither of them noticed that, at least not to the point of insisting on talking about their symptoms.

By choosing new behaviours the spouses managed to choose more connecting and less destructive behaviours at the end of the therapeutic process. They started to do more common activities, which represented a new way of appeasing their psychic needs that have been neglected for many years.

I did not pay any close attention to the daughter-in-law – mother-in-law relationship, since it turned out that there was no more need for the daughter-in-law to use conflict behaviours with her mother-in-law in order to get what she desires, as long as they, the spouses, have a connecting relationship.

This case is a presentation of the harmful use of the psychological behaviours of external control in a partner relationship. It shows a way to create new figures, through which the spouses can appease their basic psychic needs more successfully and regain control over their lives and their marriage.

Creative craziness: obsessive thoughts and compulsive actions

The choice of forced thoughts and actions is an example of the client's life being out of control, when it is impossible to turn off the creativity, but we are conscious of it. The therapeutic process with this lady, who has problems with reorganizing behaviour, represents an attempt to learn that it is not necessary to accept what our creative system offers us, if we find a more effective, organized behaviour, which helps us regain control.

Ela is a 65-year-old retired teacher of English. Nine years ago, she was hospitalized in a psychiatric clinic, because she "was hearing bells and voices and she was seeing distorted figures." She thought that "it's not normal to repeatedly check whether the gas and water are turned off, the light is off and so on." She came to a meeting with the idea that, so far, she was "maintaining" her "condition" pretty well with all the prescribed drugs and that now would be a good time to reduce the dosage of those drugs.

Regarding the medicament therapy, I directed her to the psychiatrist, because I'm not qualified for that type of questions. With some self-reflection on the situation and with a desire to change, the client has exposed her wish for a better condition. I suggested to her that we can look for things to change in her life, to do alone in order to make her feel better, if she wants that. I explained in a few words that I believe we could indirectly influence our condition with a selection of appropriate methods. I will introduce the concept of comprehensive behaviour to the client during the therapy.

When the client agreed to work to improve her feeling, taking active part, I continued the session by establishing a safe and confidential relationship, which would at the same time mean getting to know the client's world of qualities and human relations.

T: I would like to get to know you. What would you like to tell me about you?

K: I taught English at an elementary school. I loved my profession and the children too. I lived for my job at the school. I lived in a one-room flat in a small village near the city and I visited my parents every weekend. I had my vital rhythm. I don't have a herding instinct to go to places with lots of people. I'm a solitary person. I was at school most of the time. Lessons in the morning, preparations in the afternoon, clubs … in the evening I went to my friend for a chat, sometimes I watched her children. Otherwise, I kept to myself. I had a boyfriend for 8 years. We saw each other occasionally but it didn't work out. We didn't understand each other. I'm the type of person that when I get the feeling someone wants to have me only for himself, I end it. I can't stand the feeling of being controlled. I like to be alone and free. But it's just now that I feel really free, the last 2 years since my mother's death. Before that, everywhere I went, she was waiting for me at the door. When I was 15 and when I was 40. She was very afraid for me. And also, she was hoping that I would take care of in her old age. That's why she didn't want me to have my own family, because I wouldn't be able to take care of her.

T: What did you want for yourself?

K: I wanted to be able to make choices about my life, to have my mother trust me, to believe that I'm capable of making my own choices.

T: What did you want to make choices about?

K: About simple things. She didn't let me cook, go out alone with my friends.

T: Did you want that?

K: I wanted that, yes, but I always submitted to my mother's orders.

T: How so? What did you accomplish with that?

K: Probably some sort of peace, apparent peace – there weren't any conflicts between us, but I felt angry towards her and I had the feeling that I was being wronged.

T: So, if I understand, you submitted to your mother for the sake of peace, which meant a lot to you. But, if you had risked that peace, would you have acted differently? If you had risked the peace, what do you think you'd have lost in that relationship?

At this point I confronted the client with the choices she has made and the connection between her choices, and her motives and needs.

K: When I tried to do things my way, she always tightened her hold on me. I felt a lot better with my father. We all admired him. He was a pilot, strong man. Determined and severe. When he came home, there had to be total silence otherwise we were punished, even scuffled. He had a mistress, so the situation at home was a catastrophe. Then he had a stroke and my mother and I took care of him. My mother died six years after him. I lived with my mother from the first day of my retirement until her death. She was afraid to be alone, so I stayed most of the time confined in the apartment with her. I only ran to the supermarket and back and if it took me more than an hour, she was beside herself. I gave up going out with friends.

T: So, if I understand, you had to choose between the appurtenance, the love for your mother and your freedom, the affiliation with other people. And you chose the first one. Well, your mother is deceased, therefore it seems illogical to continue researching this relationship, but we can examine whether there is something familiar occurring in a present relationship that is important to you.

A brief summary about the client's family life tells us about her perception and experience of her mother's manipulation – she is a victim of controlling behaviour which she could not influence. Pondering and analysing how other people behaved, trying to control her, would not be productive, but we should not overlook the fact that she accepted this kind of behaviour and she should become aware of the motives for her choice.

Further on, I concentrated on present relationships. I followed the conviction that her mental health problems derive from difficulties in other relationships.

T: I understand from your story that you don't have a family of your own.

K: No, I don't. Later I realized that being alone suits me and besides, it's been a long time since I've been in a relationship. I have a brother. When I was a child, I wanted a brother and when he was born it was the happiest moment of my life. When I came from school, he was in his cradle and I told him everything that had happened in school. Then I drove him to the kindergarten, we've always been together. We both became teachers.

T: This kind of connection probably persists forever. How do you two get along today?

K: We've always got along. Later, our relationship was more or less severed, because I don't get along with his wife. I see my nephew 5 times a year. My brother comes to see me on his way home from work, but then he hurries home so his wife won't know that he has been visiting me.

T: How are you satisfied with these short visits? Are they enough for you?

K: No, I'm not satisfied and I suffer a lot because of that. But I don't want to have anything to do with my sister-in-law, we're too different. The two of them are my only family, but I can't get close to them.

T: What kind of relationship do you want to have with them? What do you want to be different?

K: I'd like to visit them sometimes. I have been a couple of times but I got the feeling that I wasn't welcome, so I withdrew. It's been a long time since I've been there. I'd like to go somewhere with my brother, with his family, to spend time together.

T: What would all of that mean to you? How would it make you feel?

K: I think I'd be happy and my life would have some major meaning, as well for my nephew, who I'd like to see more, but she doesn't let me.

T: Have you ever talked to your brother about what you want your relationship to be?

K: No. we both know what the problem is, but we have never actually talked about it. I'd like to talk to him, but I have never dared. I don't want to cause dissent. She's like a wolf; she keeps an eye on them and won't let them breathe. I think she doesn't want them to spend time with me because I've been in a psychiatric hospital.

There was another conviction, the belief with which the client put herself in the role of the victim, but I deliberately ignored it and concentrated on her behaviour – how she can contribute to improving their relationship.

T: I can see that the relationship with your brother means a lot to you, that you'd like to hang out more with his family, but you see your sister-in-law as someone who is preventing you from doing that. Like you said, you don't get along with her because of that. We don't know for sure what she is controlling with some manners, but we can talk about other ways for you to establish better relationships with the family despite her behaviour. What do you think?

K: I think my chances are very limited. They wouldn't let me near them. Her behaviour hurts me too much.

T: I believe it hurts you, but do you think that your relationship with her would improve spontaneously?

K: Of course not, but what can I do?! I feel so weak.

T: How can you find your strength again? What would you do, despite your sister-in-law's behaviour, to take over some sort of active role in forming a relationship with them?

K: I thought about just showing up at their home, at the door, without notifying them about my visit like I did years ago, but I realized that I'd put my brother in an unpleasant situation and that I'd only hurt him. Somehow, I didn't want to take what I wanted this way. In some way, I accept that my brother comes when he can and this is it. Probably, it's all we can have. Unless he comes to his senses and divorces that snake. But I think he would rather die than leave her.

T: Anyway, it's his decision and he will decide knowing that he's doing the best he can for himself and his loved ones. All you can do is start searching for new methods to improve the relationships with your brother and his family and to satisfy your needs. Perception is also something we choose.

Does the association of your sister-in-law with a snake help you improve the relationship with your brother?

K: (laugh)

At that point, I decide to introduce the client to the psychological needs and the methods with which we try to appease them. This is also an opportunity for the client to think about the choices she has made until now, even the bad ones.

T: ... I've already mentioned that every behaviour has its own purpose. With the choosing of the behaviour we try to appease our so-called psychological needs – to love and to be loved, to have a feeling of appurtenance, connection, to have the possibility to work in all the fields where we feel strong, competent, to be free and to have the opportunity to develop our interests, to realize our needs for knowledge, learning. These needs are common to all of us, the only difference is the way we appease them. As a matter of fact, we are constantly looking for the best ways to appease them in order to feel good.

K: And what are the needs that my sister-in-law is trying to appease?

T: I'm sure she's also trying to appease some needs. However, it's her behaviour, her "images", the figures with which she realizes herself in different roles. But I don't see any point in talking about someone else's choices, about choices we don't have any influence on. I propose we continue our conversation in the direction of searching for possibilities to appease your psychological needs. You say that you have "limited" visits with the people that mean a lot to you.

K: Yes, very limited, or it would be better to say measured out. But I was thinking right now that I also wanted to have my brother all to myself, like when we lived together and I took care of him all the time. I think I miss taking care of him, this attachment ... so this loss hurts me so much.

T: Can you compensate this loss with something else?

K: You're probably thinking about a new relationship.

T: It could be a new relationship, or you could improve the relationship with your brother, maybe connect with your sister-in-law and even get to spend time with your nephew.

K: I don't know how to connect without compromising my brother's marriage.

T: Well, I think that you didn't compromise your brother's marriage, he took care of that by himself. But you could search for methods to stay in this family under these circumstances, more connected to your brother and his family, taking into account that the relationship with your brother is very important to you, like we discussed.

K: I don't think this would do, because he's been under her influence too much and she'll never accept me.

T: Maybe their behaviour will remain the same, although if you took a different attitude in the relationship with them, this would be very improbable. How would you approach them?

K: I don't know. I don't have any hope that we could ever be close.

T: If you try with a new attitude in your relationship with them, will you have anything to lose?

K: No, but I don't see any real possibilities to change anything in our relationship.

T: You said that you took care of your brother; how can you show your care now that you're both adults or maybe take care of your nephew, your sister-in-law?

K: Concerning my nephew, I was willing to help, because he's not doing so well in school, but she wouldn't let me. She said they would solve the problem by themselves and so, I backed away.

T: If we lay aside your sister-in-law's attitude and we take into consideration the theory of choice by which no one can "direct" us if we don't want to … maybe from this point of view you can see another choice, beside the withdrawing. One that would make you feel better.

K: I don't know. I think that if I persisted there would be a conflict and I don't want that.

T: Of course, it's comprehensible. This wouldn't bring you closer.

K: Yes, although I don't want to be close to her.

T: Is it possible for you to be close to your brother and your nephew, without being close to your sister-in-law?

K: Good question. Probably not, because she controls them.

T: So, you believe that you couldn't be close to your brother, without being close to her. Are you ready to start connecting to her gradually? Or is its more acceptable for you to maintain the relationship with your brother as it is now? I also believe that you'll have some difficulties connecting with this family if you don't do anything to improve the relationship with your sister-in-law. If you want to restore some sort of relationship with her, we can talk about some methods for how to do so.

K: Yes, but nothing works with her …

T: What have you tried until now?

K: I hadn't done anything in some time, because there's no communication between us. She said that I'm dead to her, so she's dead to me.

At that point I decided, after some attempts at avoidance, to confront my client about her willingness to improve the relationship with her sister-in-law.

T: Do you even want to become closer to your sister-in law?

K: No, I didn't even want to be involved with her. It was interesting to me because of the relationship with my brother, but no, our relationship came to an end a long time ago.

T: If I understand correctly, you don't want to work on that relationship at all. But that also means the relationship with your brother won't change.

K: Let it be this way. We'll manage.

I lead the conversation from my client's position of victim and the search for causes for her misfortune in her relationships with people (her mother, brother, sister-in-law, etc.) to an active role, where she can use new choices to become close to the people she has in her quality world. But it seems that the client's belief, that "the others" are "to be blamed" for her misfortune, is firmly grounded in her and that she still accepts one's control over her and she uses that to cover her lack of engagement in taking control of her life. In the same way, she explains the relationship with her brother and her sister-in-law. In her perception, she sees her brother as a victim of his wife. I think we came to a sort of realization that she can choose her behaviour and that she can behave independently of how other people behave. But further on, we will have to work on the client's consciousness of her personal freedom.

However, we cannot overlook the fact that Ela's life story speaks about the absence of (satisfying) relationships. I think the difficulties she is confronting (creative insanity, obsessive-compulsive disorder) are closely linked to the loss of possibilities for an effective appeasement of psychological needs. The illness has interfered with her physical appearance and has made it impossible to a large extent for her to do her job– this is her "picture", which was more than just a job for her. It represented the relationships that helped her appease her needs. In this situation, the client has chosen an ineffective creative behaviour and consequently she has created a new integral behaviour, but the components are connected to one another, so the modification of one of them creates another integral behaviour. Choice theory explains that we reject the new integral behaviour when we develop more satisfying thoughts and actions. And that, in my opinion, is the purpose of the therapeutic process with Ela. She needs to judge, to understand through some self-assessment the (in) efficacy of the behaviour she chooses and to try to make better choices to gain what she really wants – her well-being.

I did not ask the client about her "strange" behaviour (the constant controlling of the gas, water …). This way, I did not let her control me by using this. I wanted her to see that she does not need it, that she does not have to accept everything the creative system offers her.

T: I remember the light in your eyes when you were talking about your job as a teacher. I felt your dedication to this profession, the love for the children … How did you experience your profession?

K: This was my life role. My mission.

T: What changed for you when you stopped teaching?

K: I'd say that a lot has changed. When you talked about the importance of relationships, I realized that leaving the place where I worked didn't just mean losing my job, but also losing all the people that meant something to me. I lost all my co-workers with whom I got along well and usually spent time with, my friends and the children, I suppose.

T: What is that you find in your relationships with the children?

K: Certainly some sort of contentment – of doing my work well, of being a good teacher; and of being loved by the children too. I had the feeling they loved me, that they accepted me, and also that they needed me. Even if this sounds bad, it was a good feeling.

T: By helping other people, we appease our need for consideration. The need for power is one of the needs we have to appease in order to feel good. You mentioned how you have appeased your need for appurtenance, acceptance, and respect, you gained new knowledge, and you had fun … in the relationships with your co-workers, the children, and your friends. Maybe we should think of how, in what way, and in which relationships you can appease your needs today?

K: I don't know. I think everything stayed there (tells the name of the village) – the work, children, colleagues. I'm not in touch with any of them. The generation of employees has changed, some of my colleagues may already have died. Here in the city, I have only my brother and a friend with whom I sometimes go to the supermarket. We talk on the phone, otherwise we don't spend time together, because she has a grandchild and she's still working. Besides my brother, there's an old woman from the neighbouring block that sometimes comes to visit me. To be honest, sometimes she is a nuisance to me.

T: Earlier we talked about your activities in your past relationships. What do you miss the most of the things you enumerated?

K: Definitely the teaching. Nothing fulfilled me like that.

T: What would it mean to you if you could teach again?

K: I think I'd feel strong, important, and useful again.

T: These definitely are not accomplishments that everybody has.

K: Yes, I agree. But just a moment later, I think that I don't know how to use them, since I don't feel alright. And all my problems.

The client's response is a typical example of trying to run from the responsibility the moment she realizes that she has the possibility to make new choices, but she is not yet ready to make an effort in order to change.

T: What problems?

K: There are a lot of them. The fear that I'll go crazy again, the fear of crowds and the dark in a hall, the fear of going into a pool. I wonder how I'll ever go into a pool; what if I fall and am a nuisance to other people? I haven't driven a car in 4 years because I was too scared. I had dizziness for a long time. I don't know whether it's because of the medicines ... The doctor thinks everything is all right. I'm not what I used to be, it's like I'm drugged.

According to Glasser's choice theory, all the symptoms, irrespective of their kind or intensity – how crazy or painful they can be – are created in order to help retain the anger that is present when we are frustrated. Ela was angry because her quality of life was diminished by an intestinal disease or rather by her perception and belief in reference to her illness. On the other hand, if she had not been controlling her anger with the symptoms, she might have thought about ending her life. But she has never talked about that because she was trying to gain some control using other ways (hallucination, auditory hallucination, compulsory acts, etc.)

We should think of these symptoms as a cry for help. The "perfect" people (Ela's mother's message to her) don't ask for help and they do not even need it. That is why she did not ask, but her symptoms were a warning. This type of expression was more acceptable for her.

We can use the symptoms to control the circumstances, so it is possible that she was getting more attention from her brother at the time (I could not say that for sure, I did not check with the client). The client was also using the symptoms to avoid the pain of unwanted and traumatic circumstances (forced retirement or a job with shorter working hours, weakness because of stoma, etc.)

I listened attentively to the client's description of her symptoms, because I believe this is very painful for her, but I did not give too much attention to this talk. I believe that all 4 components of the integral behaviour are connected to one another and that our physical health and feelings are a reflection of our deliberation and activity. That is why I wanted to find out more about the activities she engaged in during the time she was happy. She has already told me how she was successfully appeasing her basic psychic needs (teaching, working with children, spending time with co-workers …). I think this information is important for our further work. I also think it is very important for her to realize that she is "not herself anymore" when she takes the medicine. This shows us that her creativeness is not entirely paralyzed and that she wants to appease her needs.

T: Can you describe what you were like in the past? What pictures of you come to you mind when you think of that time?

K: I was happy, full of energy, and hungry for life. In the morning, on my way to school, I stopped by a friend's place for a coffee, then we went to school together, followed by classes, kids at the school, literary club in the afternoon, we were writing the gazette, a competition for the reading badge. I was full of energy, full of ideas, spirit … I never had health problems, in the last 25 years of work I took only 1 day off.

T: You were leading your life splendidly and you were making choices that made you happy, satisfied and which appeased your needs. What happened next?

K: After that, I fell ill and I had an intestinal operation. The doctor suggested that I work only 4 hours a day. The fact that I wouldn't be able to teach depressed me. What should I do in school for only 4 hours?! School was always the most important thing to me! In the same year, I started to have hallucinations and hear things. This has annihilated me. These facts were followed by my hospitalization and then vegetation from day to day.

T: I'm so sorry for what happened to you. But I'm thinking, what if you'd had the possibility to work full time, despite the doctor's suggestion – like you wanted?

K: I don't know whether at the time I gave a thought to other possibilities. It seemed right to me to follow the doctor's orders. Although it's questionable whether that decision was the best for me. After that I didn't have the will to do anything. Even today the days are all the same. In the morning, I go to the supermarket to get things for lunch; later I sit around in the apartment, watch a movie on the TV, a serial …

T: What did you like to do when you had some free time?

K: I loved reading. I've read all the juvenile books. I read 2 or 3 books per week.

T: Wow, that's a lot. Do you still read?

K: Sometimes. Less than I used to. I prefer to read magazines. I have to go to the library to get a book and I don't have enough money to buy them.

T: There's a great library in the city.

K: Yes, there is, but I'm scared. I haven't been in a library for ten years. I have some very bad memories about the library, you know. I remember that the day I went to the hospital I went into a library first. I saw a skeleton in front of me again, I heard voices ringing in my head, I didn't know where I was, who I was, I didn't know what the people looking at me were thinking. I had the feeling the ceiling would fall on me, the walls were closing on me and everything was distorted. I remember I couldn't breathe. It was horrible!

T: I believe that it has been an unpleasant experience for you. In these past years after this incident, have you ever thought about going to the library again?

K: Of course, I have thought about it lots of times. But every time I considered the possibility I started to tremble, I turned red, and I became so anxious that I gave up any thought about the library, let alone going there.

At that point I "joined the conversation professionally" and started to inform the client about the concept of integral behaviour. I kept the conversation on working with the component of thinking and activity.

T: What you have described until now is a good review of the fact that our integral behaviour is constituted of activity, thinking, feeling, and physiology and that all the components are connected. You said that just thinking about the possibility of going back to the library made you feel uneasy. Your thoughts were reflected on your body. So, I conclude that your thoughts about the library were negative. Is this correct?

K: They were full of fear. Meaning: what if I have hallucinations and I start to hear voices … what if I have to go into hospital again …

T: We can influence our state of health – our feelings exactly with the activity and view we choose. You mentioned the fear, which could have been feelings of weakness, sadness … in a word: feelings. And you mentioned the shakes, flushes … these kinds of symptoms are a reflection of our thinking and activity on our body.

K: I agree with what you said. I have already noticed several times that some thoughts can upset me, like the library, my mother's attitude, my sister-in-law … Then I have to start thinking about something else or amuse myself with something else. Most times I start watching TV and I quickly forget about unpleasant things.

T: So, you have some experience with choosing your activities and thoughts by yourself.

K: I don't know whether I'm the one choosing them.

T: You said that you interrupt the negative thoughts, followed by a bad feeling because of your integral behaviour, with a defined activity – watching television.

K: Yes, that's true, but I don't know whether I start to think about it consciously. I certainly don't want to, because it makes me upset. It seems to me that these thoughts just emerge.

T: Let's analyze your deliberation about your resumed visits to the library. You said that this kind of thoughts were full of fear until now. You also said that you don't want to be upset again, but in order to feel well you need positive and encouraging thinking. Can you think right now with me of the library in another way, a positive one?

K: You mean in the sense that I can do that, everything will be fine …

T: That's what I mean, yes. You've started well.

K: So, I can do that, everything will be fine, I haven't had any hallucinations and I haven't heard things in years, I take my medicine regularly, so why would that happen exactly in the library, now I have also a psychiatrist and a psychotherapist to help me, the counsellor from the day centre could go with me. Everything may not be as bad as I picture it, I could even enjoy being there surrounded by books …

T: How much do you believe in what you just said?

K: The phrases at the beginning – everything is o.k. etc., I don't believe them. Then I started to believe more and more that I could really do it. I mean, this way I could certainly do it. But I don't know what would happen when I really found myself in that situation. Now I felt at peace.

T: Did you notice that during your deliberation you have already started to plan the realization of the visit?

K: You are right, yes. You mean the fact with the counsellor, right?

T: Yes. Is this realizable?

K: Of course it is. The counsellors are at our disposal for cases like that.

T: Would you consider the option of asking the counsellor to accompany you?

K: I'd like her to go with me, at least the first time. She could also help me search for books among the bookshelves. It would be easier for me.

T: You'll probably regain a lot with the visit to the library regarding your love for books.

K: Yes, this is my big wish. I'm sure I would discover a new world. Maybe I'd feel a little more like myself. This would be something of mine.

The client needed support and encouragement for the visit to the library, but I tried to avoid any pressure or constraint. Nor did I lead the conversation to the formation of a concrete realization plan, because I trusted her and believed that she can accomplish this goal alone. The decision of going to the library (alone, or with the counsellor) was left to her. This way, the client received the message that she is respected and her wishes are being considered, that she does not have to do something if she does not want to and that she has the right to go to the library when she thinks it is an appropriate time. It appeared to me that the doubt about "an appropriate time" is superfluous – certainly, there have been some of these moments and they never came to realization. That's because she has identified reading books as a "picture" in her quality world and she can use it to appease her psychological needs.

In the sessions that followed I got to know other figures of Ela's quality world that she used to successfully appease her needs in the past. When she talked about the children at school and the time she spent in a village near the city, her face became serene and relaxed.

She said that her work meant everything to her. It was proved to be true when she started appeasing her needs in a destructive and painful way after losing her job (everything).

T: I think that you're managing your life much better that you did in the past. What do you think?

K: That's true. I feel a lot better and my thoughts are not as dark as they used to be. I usually get the feeling that I've never done as much for myself in my life as now.

T: Maybe this is the right time for a new step. I don't know, you tell me. We talked about the idea of you starting to teach children again and I remember you said that you would like to feel better. Now you know that our integral behaviour doesn't work that way, but it's the chosen activity that helps us feel better. Are you ready to do something with your wish – teaching others?

K: I've wanted that for a long time, it's true. I think that if I did it again I'd choose to teach English.

T: I was thinking of lectureship and translation, too, but I think teaching is a better choice. It could help you start new relationships. Your knowledge is precious and there are a lot of children that have problems studying English.

K: English is one of the most difficult subjects, in the elementary school too. As for the lectureship and translation, I wouldn't do that because I don't have any experience with that.

T: I understand. So, you'd try teaching, would you?

K: Yes, I think there's a need for teachers and the job is well paid, so I could improve my pension.

T: Yes, great. Do you have any idea how to offer your services, how to get students?

K: My brother is a teacher, so he could recommend me. He used to ask me if I'd teach someone, but I always turned him down.

T: Are you ready for this new experience? Do you have any doubt about this and would you like to talk about it?

K: I think I should start with one student, not more.

T: As you wish. It's your choice and your decision. We'll keep having sessions, so if you wanted to talk about anything, there wouldn't be a problem.

K: This helps me a lot. I feel a little agitated, but it's not the same type of agitation that makes me feel bad, I'm fine now. I have started to think about the arrangements and a place to teach in, there are some things that need to be finalized.

T: Would you like to talk about something, to think about it together?

K: Not really. I'm coming to conclusions regularly and there hasn't been any major problem. I'm glad, I feel positive again and I'm feeling well.

Soon, she started giving lessons, which turned out to be a good choice for a new behaviour, because this job makes her feel successful. She is aware of the fact that she is a good teacher and so she is successfully appeasing her needs for strength, freedom (she is the one deciding how many students she will have and when), and amusement (she is renewing her old knowledge and learning new things). At the end of the consultancy she had two children and she was happy with that. She got close to the mother of a girl she is teaching (they exchange gifts for holidays and birthdays, they go out together), she is working hard at new relationships.

I expected that as a teacher she is familiar with the psychology of external control (she also said that she mostly used anger with the children for "good purpose") and that these new relationships with her students would improve with the help of her new knowledge of choice theory.

Through the advisory process, she was gaining more and more control over her life. The two of us were close enough that I could start a conversation about new relationships.

I'm presenting a part of our conversation about partnership.

[...]

K: I dated my last boyfriend for 8 years. We didn't live together; we were just seeing each other. He was violent towards me just once. It was pretty bad; I avoided people for some time. I didn't tell my mum at all, because it would have hurt her too much.

T: Did you ask for help?

K: No, I was too ashamed. Actually, I haven't told anyone.

T: How do you live with that?

K: I have locked it somewhere inside of me, like it didn't happen. But since then I've been more careful with men.

T: What are your relations with men these days?

K: Pretty reserved. Actually, I don't want to be with anyone.

T: Why's that?

K: Because I have a plastic bag (she had an intestinal operation – note Podgornik). I had a correspondence with an Englishman named John and when he asked to meet me, I wrote back to him: "I've got a plastic bag now and I don't want to write letters to you anymore". He wrote back: "What about the plastic bag?" I didn't answer him. We had been writing to each other for 10 years, I wrote him poems, I recorded my letters onto tapes and he commented on my English. But when he asked to meet me, the correspondence stopped. When I got that message, I didn't want to have any contact with him again.

T: I think his answer meant more something like, what should this mean to me?! So, he accepts it and nothing has changed for him.

K: I think that too, but I keep imagining what his reaction would be when he saw me. I don't want anyone to feel sorry for me.

T: We don't know what other people would do. We just know what our actions would be and we can just assume for others. What would you do if he had a stoma? Would you accept that?

K: It's difficult to say, I don't know, I'd probably accept it.

T: What would you have lost if you had taken a risk and continued your relationship with John?

K: I'd have lost my dignity. His rejection would have humiliated me.

T: This can be bad. Would this be the worst that could have happened?

K: Yes, this would have been the worst for me.

T: Would this have been worse than losing the relationship and, as a matter of fact, you don't even know if it was really necessary?

K: Obviously I was afraid that his words would just confirm what I already know – that I look awful with the bag. Believe me, it's terrible to see.

T: Yes, I understand that the bag is something bad for you and that you didn't want to risk showing it to someone. I don't have any experience with that and so I can't know what I would be feeling, but I had some scars on my stomach and I "tortured" myself with the question whether my partner would accept me. But this was my problem really, not his. He was showed some compassion for me, because of my bad experience, but that's all. My sewn stomach has never been a problem and our sexuality wasn't less beautiful. But it was me who had to change my perspective. Maybe these thoughts will help you. I also know that in a loving relationship this kind of thing becomes insignificant. To stay in this context, I'd like to know whether you still want a loving and intimate relationship but you're too afraid, or you don't even want it?

K: It's difficult, because after the operation I decided to remain alone and I really don't have any wish for a man. No offence, it has nothing to do with you, but I don't want to talk about it, because I wouldn't change my mind.

T: You have the right to make that choice. I suggest that if you ever want to talk about it with me, just tell me. Would that be OK for you?

K: I agree, it's easier now that we have settled that, because I don't want to talk about it.

At this point, the client has exposed another dysfunctional belief which makes it impossible to have new relationships. The "bag" represents an obstacle which she uses as a protection because of her fear of intimacy.

During the counselling process, I offered her some knowledge about choice theory, I informed her about some literature that we talked about, and about good relationships for the sake of her mental health. She "equipped" herself with some new knowledge from choice theory and someday she will may get close to someone in a relationship and appease her needs more successfully.

This is the third year of Ela coming to me for consultations; in the last year there have been only some occasional conversations – when she knows her creative system is working again in a destructive way and she needs help to gain control over her life – but she still sticks to the idea of not having any relationships, saying that she does not need them.

The fact that in this time the client has developed other relationships with which she can appease her physical needs is very positive. Regarding the unsatisfying relationship with her brother and his wife, she decided to establish a relationship with her nephew (at the end of the school year she gave him a book with a dedication; all three together (she, her brother and her nephew) went to the cemetery to visit and commemorate the grandparents, and spent an afternoon during summer by the River Soča. She expressed her satisfaction and she thinks this is more than she hoped for. She considered getting in touch with her nephew more often, because she saw that he accepted her.

Our relationship can also represent for her some sort of satisfying relationship. We talked about that. In the relationship she has with me, she can appease some psychological needs (especially the need for acceptance, appurtenance, and partially the need for strength and amusement) and it helps her keep control over her life. I think it was because of this relationship that I was able to manage this therapeutic process, because she was coming regularly to therapy and she participated actively in the process, despite the fact that I did not "succumb" to the attempt to control me with her symptoms.

She frequently thanks me for passing her the knowledge that helps her and for talking with her like she was "completely normal". This certainly means a lot to me, but it is also important (to me) that in this relationship I have satisfyingly appeased my needs too – in spite of the client's apparent severity and her "didactic" attitude, there was a lot of warmth, acceptance, and approval.

Through the therapeutic process, I could see in what terms she saw herself. Her beliefs about herself reflected her lack of self-confidence, of confidence in her abilities, unacceptability, not appreciating herself as she is, inequality in relationships with others, etc. That is why we worked even on the basic relationship, the relationship with oneself. Ela talked about memories of her mother, who always said she could have done better when she came home with a good report, despite the excellent results. "You can always do better", that was one of the beliefs Ela used to pressure herself. To be the best, to be perfect ... this is the burden she still carries within herself. We are still working on self-kindness, on an understanding attitude towards herself, when she does not succeed in something, and when she is not "the best". It seems that the most difficult thing for Ela is changing her attitude towards herself.

Otherwise, during all the years we have been having these sessions, she has done so much for herself. Every day she takes an hour's walk, regardless of the weather and her condition. Once a week she goes to aqua aerobics. She takes part in the activities organized by the day centre (especially the hikes and occasional trips). In summer, she spends most of the days at the city pool with her colleagues from the day centre. She has started to read a lot again, to teach, etc. Through the therapeutic process, she has replaced her reorganized creativity – the insanity with a new and simple organized behaviour and so she has regained her control. But further on, she should change her position of being a victim of her bag, in order to enter an intimate relationship. The position of victim makes it impossible for her to make a choice and this leads to a poor possibility of satisfying her needs for freedom in intimacy. Probably, she uses this "bag" to cover up some deeper fears, but only their removal would mean a lot more freedom for the client.

Addiction (to sex)

Sex addiction is a modern form of addiction and like other forms, it represents an attempt to find satisfaction outside mutual relationships. This is why the counselling-therapeutic work with the client who has this kind of problems, is focused on learning new forms of behaviour, with which he can renew old relationships and create new ones. With the relationships the client finds satisfying, he can find pleasure even with normal life satisfactions, which last longer than the pleasure given by intoxication.

I present an example of psychotherapy with a client who tries to alleviate or reduce a painful frustration in his life by getting intoxicated.

I received a phone call from Alen, a forty-five-year-old male, who expressed the desire to come for a talk. He told me that he thinks he is a sex addict, because during the last year he has completely focused on it, while neglecting other responsibilities and activities.

I remember the client's uneasiness and embarrassment at our first meeting. The introduction at the beginning of the session was a little longer than usual, with the intention of building a connective relationship in order to help him relax and feel that I accept him, regardless of the problems that brought him to me.

The client came to the first meeting with a prepared self-estimation, having perceived the problem as dedicating to much of his time to sex, and the realization that it affects his well-being and quality of life.

I present the client's presentation and interpretation of his problems with the self-evaluation, with which he come to therapy.

T: Could you tell me more about the problems you're currently facing, please?

K: I'm realizing that all my thoughts are connected to sex. I have these thoughts all the time and I can't stop them. I can't break from this vicious circle. I can't see the exit. Recently, I read an article about sex addiction and in an instant my eyes opened. That's it. That's happening to me. I'm addicted to sex! Not even to sex, but to erotica. I don't like pornography. I get excited by looking at erotic images, I'm obsessed with that and I can do it for hours, all day. In those moments, my body is tense, it's difficult to describe, it's like it would explode if I didn't get satisfied, but after I regain control, after I calm down, I feel terrible. Even this calm that I regain doesn't last long, I soon become confused, restless, if I could I would just run away …

T: I believe it can't be pleasant for you. What was your intention when you decided to come to this session? What do you want for yourself, for your life?

K: I feel bad because of what I'm doing. I think I need help, but I don't see how could I get rid of that, since it's accessible to me all the time and I don't have the strength to resist it.

T: I believe that with time you'll gain that strength. In that I actually find the meaning of therapy and my role. In the fact that I stand beside you, when you're facing your problems and that I help you find new, better choices for yourself. I'd like to know what are you expecting from therapy, what is it that you think you need help with and how can I help you?

K: I want to talk with you about my problems without restraint, because I have no one in my life that I can trust, complain to about what bothers me. I'm afraid that people would laugh at me, devalue me. Actually, it has already happened and I was very hurt by it.

T: I can assure you that I will treat your situation professionally and conscientiously, like any other situation that make people suffer and because of which people come to me to talk. I'd like to say that everything we talk about will remain confidential, I'm bound by the ethical code, and without your consent I won't even use it for my studies and professional purposes. I'm bound to promise you that, it's my responsibility.

K: I trust you, it's alright. I was thinking, actually I realized that I just fall back to this behaviour when I have a hard time. At that time, there's a force pushing me towards erotica to satisfy myself, get intoxicated and function more easily. At least I thought, I hoped that I would function better, and maybe at the beginning I did, but now it's getting more difficult. Recently my condition hasn't been good. I think I'm suffering. It's difficult to admit to myself, I'd prefer if it was all just for pleasure and not my nightmare. Except for my work, I don't do anything useful. All the time I think about the next chance to look at those things.

Further on I'll be asking the client questions that will lead to unrealized "pictures", images he keeps in his personal album – quality world, because, according to choice theory, there are unsatisfied psychic needs behind the client's destructive behaviour.

T: You say that you use this kind of behaviour when you feel bad. What do you connect this feeling with? What do you miss in that moment?

K: I don't know how to explain it. It looks like nothing special is happening, at least I don't notice anything happening. But I feel somehow empty, hollow, I feel a kind of general sadness, emptiness inside of me.

T: Do you connect your behaviours with an event, dissatisfaction that you perceived in yourself or your marriage, family, perhaps?

K: No, I don't remember anything happening that would make me occupy myself so intensively with it. But everything started in my childhood. If I remember correctly, I was around six, when I started to masturbate. I had been interested in sex for quite some time, I'd say that I was more interested in it than my peers were. I don't even know if I'm actually addicted to sex or I'm just getting panicked over nothing.

At this point I was not ready to discuss the doubt around whether he is addicted or not, nor the question "Do others do that as well?". The question of what makes a person an addict also did not seem like an appropriate next step for a successful therapy session. The only relevant information is that the client does not feel good about the selection of his behaviour, that he cannot appease in an effective way his psychic needs. A person's well-being is the signal (scale) that informs our organism about whether we manage to live in line with a desired image from our quality world or not.

Further on I tried to expand the context from symptomatology to relationships, because the client still cannot link his problems with relationship problems, when the lack of good relationships is substituted with hedonism. I continued the discussion that led the client to self-estimation. I expect that the therapeutic process will proceed so that the client reinforces his confidence in himself, in his capacities, and that the new choices he makes in life will help him do things that will give him a sense of pleasure and satisfaction, without being followed by pain.

T: Do you have a partner or a family?

K: Yes, I have a family. My wife knows everything, I don't hide anything from her, because she doesn't judge me. I'm embarrassed that she has such a wuss for a husband, I'm also embarrassed because of my daughters. I know that they know something but I have never talked with them about that.

T: Does this mean that your behaviour is somehow separating you from others?

K: Yes, it's like a huge gap between me and my wife; even if we don't mention it, we both know that it's there. I'm also sure that my older daughter kind of knows and she resents me for my behaviour. I have also thought that she may find me disgusting, even if nothing has ever been said about it. Now that I think of it, I realize that everyone in the family knows but no one wants to talk about it. Maybe because of that the situation at home can be awkward sometimes. Of course it's awkward.

T: This is an important realization that you and your loved ones are not alright. If you agree, next time I'd like to continue our discussion about the relationships that are important for you. I think it's enough for the first time.

K: Yes, it's enough. To tell you the truth, at first I thought that it would be easier to talk about my problems with a male therapist. Explaining those things to a woman would be more difficult.

T: How do you feel after our first talk?

K: I feel fine, I'm calm. I'd like to come to you again. I wanted to say that at first I had this doubt but I don't anymore.

T: In any case, you have the right to have a male therapist. This decision is completely acceptable for me. But I'd like to inform you that from now on the therapy won't be focused on the discussion of sexuality, if that's what's making you uncomfortable. It's good for me to know how you understand, experience your problems, what your activities are regarding those problems, and that's all. Drawing from the theory, I know that addictions are a consequence of having dissatisfying relationships, which we realized in a part of our discussion. I suggest that next time we focus on your relationships, behaviours, your life activities. What do you think? Do you believe that your problems may be somehow linked to your relationships?

K: I don't know, maybe. Before we were discussing the fact that the situation at home is not the best and maybe it's logical that I wouldn't have such strange needs if I were completely satisfied with my life.

T: Do you agree that next time we'll take a look at your relationships?

K: I agree.

The client described his total behaviour beautifully and the inevitable interaction between individual components (keeping himself busy with the thought and/or activity, followed by physiology and feelings). There is a true range of emotions – from pleasure, comfort, pace to feelings of guilt, inferiority, powerlessness, incapacity, etc.

The client has already experienced the deceitfulness of an addiction (even if non-chemical), which means that the "drug" has already started to lessen and the client is experiencing the pain that represents the loss of control. Regardless of that, he still keeps a false sense of control, because he has not yet managed to develop more satisfying ways of appeasing his basic needs. During the therapy, we will try to understand which is the variable (an incompatibility between the reality he perceives and the internal instructions about which reality is the best for surviving) that he controls.

Virtual erotica gives Alen easy access to pleasure, which influences the chemical activity of the brain and the information that at least one of the basic human needs has been appeased. The fact is that with this kind of intoxication Alen tries to reduce the pain of frustration in his life.

The purpose of the therapeutic work with Alen is to help him develop ways that would help him reach the same kind of pleasure that he has already experienced. These new ways would help him enjoy everyday life satisfactions that last longer and truly appease one of the basic human needs, because he would be appeasing it through relationships with his loved ones. With this kind of appeasing of his needs, he will give up his old way of intoxication, because he will no longer need it.

The client realizes the destructive power of addiction, he is ready to change his behaviour, which would ensure a better, stronger future with his family.

Perhaps, during our next session we took a step back in searching for more satisfying choices, but I was following the client and his needs in that moment. Within the frame created by the client, I oriented the discussion towards choice theory.

K: Last time, when we talked about the time it all started, I started thinking. I remember the fights between my parents, especially when my father came home drunk and yelled at me and my mother ... he was often very violent to both of us, especially my mother. Then I went to my room to have some peace, to hide from what was happening. I think that I masturbated in order to comfort myself, as if the pain would lessen. But these fights were quite frequent since my father was an alcoholic, and because of that I masturbated regularly. If I think back, what a mess was at home!

T: I'm sorry that you had such a sad childhood.

K: Luckily my father died not long after and it was just me and my mother. I don't know whether it was soon after, I was just fifteen at the time, but the damage was already done.

T: Before your father died, did you manage to get somehow closer with him?

K: No, there was no way. When I reached puberty, I started to withstand him, I defended my mother as much as I could. He died quickly, we didn't say goodbye.

T: Today you're an adult. How do you explain your father's behaviour?

K: I think he was a wuss, who couldn't take care of his family. He didn't respect his wife, he was never satisfied with me, I was just a brat in his way. I don't have any good memories, nothing good ties me to my father.

T: Would it be easier for you if you were to look in a different way at his behaviour, which was painful for you and for which there is no apology?

K: How could I look at it differently!?

T: I was thinking that maybe those were extremely unsuccessful attempts for him to be considered, respected. I know that it was these behaviours that made him lose everything, but some people mistakenly think that precisely violence and other forms of compulsive behaviour can guarantee the love of our loved ones, their acceptance.

K: I think that he could see in my eyes that I despised him. I waited with him for hours after school in a bar, so that he would later take me home. I was ashamed of him and he had to know that, because I showed him that. My mother was afraid of him. I could see the fear in her eyes, the fear that he'd do something to me too.

T: How would you describe their relationship in other words?

K: My mother didn't love him. There was no affection between them. I often thought that in reality he was an unhappy man, but I didn't know why, what had happened in his life.

T: Maybe he couldn't establish a better relationship with the people he loved – with you and your mother?

K: This kind of thinking makes me want to cry. I feel sorry for him, instead of the anger that I always felt when I thought of him.

T: I remember a therapist that talked about "a wardrobe of resentments". In this room, we keep all our painful events, resentments towards others, and by reviving them we just create more pain for ourselves. Could you imagine having each of these resentments on you like a shirt that you could just take off and throw it on the floor like an old shirt when you don't want or like it anymore? And just like that, you could take your resentments off your shoulders one by one. Then you walk out of that wardrobe of resentments and you close the door behind you, leaving all the resentments inside. Would it be easier for you, if you could deal with your resentments this way?

K: Right now, just as I was listening to you, I could see before my eyes scenes, literally see the scenes, people with whom I don't want to deal anymore. My shoulders really would feel lighter. I think my past is my burden.

T: This "wardrobe of resentments" is one of the ways to deal with resentments. It's about our perception of something that could have a different form, one that could be easier for us, as we talked before about your perception about your father's behaviour.

K: I've never thought this way. My only belief was that the facts were as I knew them to be, that my view was the only one possible, that others didn't exist.

T: You'll see, perhaps these things, which we talked about today, will help you with your "flashbacks". But Alen, do you think that "looking back" to your past, reliving it, helps you in any way in resolving the problems you're facing today?

K: I don't know. Now I have problems with myself, in the past I had them with my father. Maybe the cause of my problems is hidden in my childhood.

T: Maybe. How could this realization help you solve your current problems?

K: Well, I'd like to know what the real cause of my problems is.

T: You'd like to know that the cause of your problems originated in your childhood. You may also like to know who's responsible for the problems you're facing today. But I still don't know how these realizations could help you solve your current problems, i.e. an excessive use of virtual erotica.

K: I don't know. I thought that you'd know something about that.

T: (smile) I don't have this magic wand. What happened to you can't be deleted. I'm sorry. But we can look at your past in the light of choice theory. Choice theory explains that past traumatic experiences could have left determined consequences on us, but it doesn't help us in treating them today, it just helps to make us feel better, to live happily and contentedly here and now. The cause of our current unhappiness is in the present, in our present relationships, or because of the lack of them. So, if you agree, next time we could talk about your current relationships with others.

K: Yes, I agree. Until our next session I'll think about my relationships.

I link the client's frustrating experiences in his early childhood to his "resorting" to sexuality, to something that gives him comfort, as an attempt to appease his needs. The way of manifesting his distress could also be connected to the fact that he was physically and mentally abused as a child. But we did not stop at the client's information about the abuse. According to Glasser, reliving and confronting abuse during the therapeutic process is not just ineffective, but also harmful. On the other hand, for others, especially in psychoanalytic approaches, it is necessary. Telling people that they are victims and that they cannot help themselves is extremely harmful. Choice theory explains that it is important for the clients to realize that they suffer because of the loss of trust in people, they were hurt by the people of their quality world. Alen needs a satisfying relationship with someone he can trust.

Because our behaviour is intentional, we believe that preserving and repeatedly reliving the past and anchoring ourselves in the roles of victims have some sort of purpose. I did not want to roughly interfere with this belief, but I lightly allowed it in order to maintain the relationship and the client's gradual learning to take responsibility.

The axiom of choice theory explains that a person, regardless of the traumatic events he experienced in his childhood, is not a victim of his past, unless he chooses to be. In order to relieve the client's distress, there's a question that needs to be answered – how could he now, in his actual life period, appease his needs and live a satisfying life.

I listened to the client when he expressed the desire to talk about painful events from his childhood and youth. I used the client's story in order to interpret and implement choice therapy – with what purpose we choose a determined behaviour, what drives us and the fact that our well-being does not depend on someone else's behaviour, and what we can really influence in our life.

We gradually passed to the study of the relationships with his loved ones and we determined the level of satisfaction with the existing relationships. Alen described his mother as the only adult person with whom he was able to connect while growing up. This is why I was not surprised that this relationship was the first that came to mind, even if he has not lived with his mother for a long time, and Alen now has a family of his own. But perhaps he is still searching for the causes of his present unhappiness in his difficult upbringing.

K: When you talked about relationships last time, I thought of my mother. It's interesting because she's not such a big part of my life now.

T: Is the relationship with your mother the one you'd like to focus on now?

K: I'd like to talk about it. I think there's something that I need to resolve here.

T: Alright. How do you see your relationship now?

K: My mother and I, we were always allies. I know why. I know she did the maximum for me that she could in those conditions. If I haven't had a mother like her, it would have been much worse for me. She saw to it that I was always tidy and that we looked like a normal family as much as possible. I don't resent my mother for any of that. On the other hand, she was always very demanding towards me, it was difficult for me to reach her standards, even as a child. She wanted me to be very good in school, but I didn't like studying and because of that I was under pressure. Even today, she still pressures me to get an education, to be successful, important. Now I just tell her to get lost, I don't let her annoy me.

T: Have you ever talked with your mother about her desire for you to have a good education?

K: Not at all. I tried more to resist that than try to find out why she is so insistent about that. Like, I can be a good person only if I have an education.

T: I was thinking that your mother must have seen in your education a possibility for a better future for you. So that your life would be easier, that you might have more opportunities than she had. This is just my thought, maybe you can check it by talking to her.

K: Maybe we could really have an opportunity to talk about it. What you say is very possible. I realize that I tried my best, even at home when possible, to be a good and obedient child, so there were no fights, or that my father didn't scream because of me. But I also realize that I'll never be the son she wishes me to be.

T: How do you see yourself in the role of a son? What kind of son would you like to be?

K: I think I'm not grateful enough for what my mother did for me. In reality, I'd like be more attentive towards her.

T: How do you imagine this attention towards your mother?

K: By visiting her more. I don't go see her very often and I know I could do that more frequently.

T: What would it mean for you to visit her more often? In that case, would you feel more like the son you want to be?

K: I think I would. I think I'd have the feeling of having behaved as she expects me to and that would make her happy.

T: Would that make you happy too?

K: I think it would. Somewhere inside of me I feel that I miss her, that she's an important person for me.

T: Do you have the possibility to visit her more?

K: Yes, I have time, that's not a problem. My wife often tells me to invite my mother for lunch, but I'm not up for it. I think that I simply never realized the need to spend more time with my mother.

T: I believe that every choice of our behaviour has its own meaning, we want to achieve something with it. Perhaps by getting closer to your mother you would gain something for yourself?

K: Maybe I'd feel better because I'd be doing something for her. I know I feel useful when I visit her and bring her food or anything else she may need. I feel a warmth inside, a nice feeling, which I also have when I do something good for my girls at home.

T: I think it's good that you recognize, as you do now, what makes you happy and you use it more frequently.

K: Yes, I believe it would be good for all of us, for my daughters too, to visit my mother more often. I think my wife tries to do more for her than I do.

T: You mentioned some ways you could use to get closer. Maybe you could have a think, opt for one and then do it.

K: I'll talk with my wife; I'd like to invite my mother to our house for lunch.

T: Can we talk more concretely about your contribution regarding your mother's visit, so we can prevent the fact that it would be mostly your wife who is paying attention to her?

K: I agree but nothing good about what could I do comes to my mind. My wife cooks and the girls help her. I would bring my mother and maybe this time I could help her up the stairs, not my wife, I could talk more with her about her health, listen more to what she has to say. Maybe something else, I'll think about it.

T: Do you recognize these behaviours, the ones that you were thinking about just now, as possible ways of getting closer to your mother, to connect with her, to have a tighter relationship?

K: I think, I do. When I think about these possibilities I feel good. It seems like I started doing something with my life, to do more planning, only after I started coming to these meetings with you.

T: I don't understand what you mean by saying that you just have started doing something with your life.

K: Until now I lived just like that. Things just happened without me doing something about it. I never planned anything. I'm not responsible enough for that. I'm sort of a do-nothing type, if something happens, then it's OK, if not, that's alright too. I realize that I've had a lot of luck in my life, since everything has turned out alright.

T: Can you tell me what turned out so fine, without you having anything to do with it, if I understand you correctly?

K: Everything that has happened in my life; my family, work, our house.

T: All that happened without you?

K: (laugh) I never planned any of this, I didn't have any influence on the ways things have turned out.

T: Who had this influence then?

K: I don't know, it's difficult to say. I think it was a set of circumstances, because I don't think of myself competent enough to make something happen, even if I tried to.

Listening to the client, it is possible to understand that he does not perceive himself as a co-creator of the important events in his life; even more, he perceives these events as occurrences on which he did not have any influence, he understands them as a reflection of some external factors, acting independently of him. I believe that behind this way of thinking there is a person who does not have a positive opinion of himself, does not recognize (does not realize and consequently cannot value) his skills and talents, and does not believe in his capacities and abilities (choosing, creating, actualizing, etc.) He probably does not have an active approach to life, and therefore he does not need to take responsibilities. As such or with this kind of beliefs, he cannot successfully appease his psychic needs in his relationships with others. Since we all want to be successful, important, respected, accepted, and loved (according to Glasses, our genetic code dictates that), I assume that Alen's real picture about himself differs strongly from his ideal one and maybe that is the variable he tries to control with his behaviours (intoxication with sexuality, the so-called social phobia – I found out about it during the next conversation), which he believes would give him the desired (picture of himself).

T: Alen, I'd like to know how you see and perceive yourself. What's your opinion about yourself? How do you see yourself in your role of husband, father, son, friend?

K: I think you already realized that my opinion is not so good. I believe I still carry inside of me the sense of inferiority I gained as a child. Even now, after all these years, I can hear my mother telling me that I will accomplish nothing in life. I simply believe that I'm not good enough or not as good as others. You know, around two years ago, I started stammering in front of others, I just couldn't talk and I had a feeling in my head that I was about to pass out. Very unpleasant. Then I started avoiding others. My wife and I almost stopped hanging out with friends. Last time we went on a picnic, some friends invited us, but I couldn't relax. All that time I was thinking what would happen if someone asked me something, would I be able to utter anything, say something normal. Maybe it seems funny, but after an event like that I feel completely beaten, drained. My wife knows about my problems and she also knows that I want her besides me all the time, because she makes it easier for me – if I have a problem, she jumps in (laugh). In reality, this situation is very painful for me. Because of that I suffer and avoid people. Last time I saw an ex-classmate from way back who'd had much more success in life than I have, I just went in the other direction. I don't know how it would have been if I'd met him and I couldn't talk. Anyway, there are a lot of stories like this one.

T: What were your first thoughts when you saw this classmate, if we remain on this example?

K: Thoughts? I don't even know whether I actually think of something in this kind of situation. I just look around to find an escape route.

T: First, there's a thought and then the action follows. Before you talked about signals, about how you feel distress. I'd like to know what happens before that. If you try to remember, what was your first thought?

K: Something like: "Not him. How can I have a conversation with him, I won't be able to manage it. I will feel like fainting, I'll sweat and stammer. He's successful, he acts all superior, and he's inaccessible. What if he asks me what I do in life?"

T: And your answer would have been?

K: I'd say something quickly, just to get it over with, like: "I'm struggling on my own. For now, it's alright."

This kind of thinking surely does not help Alen to develop a sense of belonging, a connection with others. The current choice of behaviour shows a loss of control over his life and the use of controlling behaviours. Therefore, further on we will work on some ways to connect with others.

T: OK. And how would you like to answer him, how would you like to behave with him?

K: Well, I'd talk sovereignly, decisively. It'd be good if I had anything to say, like that I'd finished my studies while working, that I have my own company, and that I'm successful (laugh).

T: And how would you feel with that kind of performance?

K: I think that would be very good. It'd be fantastic if I could manage that.

T: How would you think and see yourself in that situation?

K: I think I'd say to mysel, that I'm very good, a nice person, who can communicate with others. I'd say something like that.

T: What's stopping you now from saying this to yourself and presenting yourself as you want to?

K: That's not me. I can't behave like that.

T: Who decides about the way you behave?

K: Me probably, but I don't feel like I'm the one deciding.

T: Choice theory explains that a person alone has the power to choose his thoughts and actions and with that choice he indirectly influences his well–being – the physiology and emotions. It's not the contrary, the treating of symptoms a person has doesn't influence his well–being.

K: You're saying that I decide about what I do?

T: Of course, regarding what you want. As I said, all our behaviours have their purpose. When you talked about your life events, you certainly helped create them. If their creation wasn't in your interest, you wouldn't attempt them and wouldn't succeed. I'm sure you have some skills, capacities, talents. Maybe you could think about what you're good at, what your qualities are, what makes you happy, what you like to do, etc., until next time. What do you say?

K: Alright. I have never thought about my qualities, maybe I really am too self-critical and I mostly see the things where I have didn't succeeded in life – mostly the fact that I only finished vocational school.

T: While thinking, try to focus on your qualities.

The client's story tells us that during his childhood and youth he did not have enough images in order to successfully appease his psychic needs, which he experiences as an adult. His father's love was conditioned, so was his mother's (with successes and diligence). Alen admits that his mother did everything she could, she always tried to hide form him the discords with his father and to make the situation easier for him. He, as her child, tried to please her – to be good in school and at home, not causing any additional problems, believing in the principle "stimulus-reaction". The presence in the quality world was mutual and strong, so that helped Alen, as an adult, with different ways of appeasing his psychic needs (family, care for his loved ones).

Alen still experiences controlling behaviours from his mother, while he describes his wife as extremely understanding. He is convinced that he does not deserve such a good wife, who values him more than he deserves, and who would be certainly disappointed if she knew about his thoughts and actions. At this point his belief about himself emerges, which is not in line with his desired self-image.

I believe that with those negative beliefs about himself and his actions, the client influences the formation of feelings of loneliness, isolation from his loved ones. Falling back into the world of virtual sexuality cannot save him from his loneliness and disconnection and this is why he remains unhappy. His behaviour may bring him momentary pleasure, satisfaction, also the feeling of power and capacity, otherwise he would not use it so regularly, but it cannot bring him a sense of happiness. In order to be happy, he needs to establish relationships with people and not virtual persons. This is why further on we paid more attention to the improvement of existing relationships, more specifically the relationship with his partner, and we focused on the appeasing of some unappeased psychic needs.

T: Alen, you mentioned your wife and your daughters. I thought that today we could talk about the relationships in your family.

K: Yes, we can. I'd like to say that I'm not married to Tanja. Even if we've been together for twenty years, we have never decided to marry.

T: O. K. How would you describe your relationship?

K: I'd describe it as good. I think that we work very well together.

T: Can you tell me a bit more about what a good relationship means to you?

K: We don't have big fights and in general we don't fight very much, because she's very adapting, diligent, obliging, she's not a demanding woman, she also doesn't nag. I mean, she would sometimes be justified, because I can be difficult, but she always tries to smooth everything.

T: How do you perceive her, satisfied or not so much?

K: Well, I thought about it last time. The allergies she started to have recently also made me think that they may be connected to our relationship. I think I pressure her too much, that I harass her unnecessarily. You know, I thought about the fact that her allergies are merely a consequence of her not expressing her dissatisfaction, last time her face was all swollen.

T: Do you ever talk about it? What's Tanja's opinion about your relationship? How does she see it?

K: It's difficult to say what she thinks, because we don't talk about it. I think that's precisely what she misses in our relationship – talking about our satisfaction, our well-being. I have always preferred to avoid that.

T: How would you check your thinking and expectations about her feelings?

K: Well, by talking to her.

T: Are you prepared to talk?

K: I am, even if it's very awkward. But it really is the only way to find out.

T: If we go back to your relationship, is there anything you miss in your relationship with Tanja?

K: Of course there is. Our relationship is somehow tepid, nothing special, lately I've realized that everything has become just a routine.

T: If I understand correctly – your life together has become a routine?

K: Yes, our life, but especially our sex life. I know that my sexual needs are bigger than those of other men and hers. I admit that she pleases me in many ways, but I'd like more. I'm not satisfied anymore with our sexual life, really not. I know that I can say everything here. I trust you. There's a thought more and more present, I frequently think about having an affair.

T: What do you want to gain? What would an affair mean to you?

K: I think I need something new, passion. I don't know whether I'd really go through with it. I also think that I don't have the courage to do that, that I'm a sort of sissy, who only dreams, but doesn't dare.

T: Would you then feel less like a sissy and more like a man?

K: Maybe.

T: Are you ready to risk the good relationship you have at home for that?

K: I think I'm not. Because I don't trust myself enough. I'm afraid I would lose control and I'd lose my family. I don't know if I could pretend, I'm too emotional. I'm afraid I'd fall in love and my emotions would drag me into a passionate relationship. But I can't imagine my life without Tanja.

T: What's so good in this relationship that it makes you want to keep it?

K: It gives me a sense of security, comfort. Certainl, also the fact that she accepts me as I am. In any case, I want to keep her. But I'm also tempted by an affair, I confess.

T: Do you think that an affair would still tempt you if you were more satisfied and you were to revive your relationship?

K: Maybe not.

T: Could you find or revive what you're searching for in your relationship with Tanja?

K: You mean passion?

T: Yes, everything you say that makes you unsatisfied – the routine, tepidness … Are you still attracted to her?

K: Yes, I am. Although she's not a very attractive woman, I'd say she's a normal, classic type of woman. I realize that she can't become a tall, long-legged blonde, but she has other qualities. This term you use is very well-chosen – qualities!

T: Do you have any special qualities in mind?

K: She always tries very hard, even in bed. She's more of a romantic soul. She wants everything soppy. She likes little attentions, she's really happy when I get her flowers once a year.

T: Do you want to improve your marriage? Are you ready to do something in order to feel more satisfied in this relationship?

K: You're trying to tell me that I should try to be more romantic. I know that because she's been reproaching me about it since we've been together, but I'm not that kind of man.

T: Do you remember when we talked about the fact that we choose our behaviours? You can be the type you want to be.

K: Yes, I remember. I could be more attentive, she deserves that.

T: I believe that your wife deserves many things and I think it's nice that you're thinking about it, but as we said earlier, you have to talk with her about it, we could just guess or presume what part of your marriage dissatisfies her. You said that you're not completely satisfied with this relationship, that you want a better relationship for you and that you're ready to do something for it. Did I understand that correctly?

K: Yes, it's true.

T: Perhaps we could think together about how to improve your relationship, so you'll feel better, more satisfied in this relationship.

K: Yes. I'd like to know how to stop this routine, because I think it's killing me.

T: Could you describe what you imagine as a routine?

K: I think about my daily routine – in the morning going to work, then home, working around the house, once a year a week of holidays at the beach, that's all my life. Do you understand what I'm trying to say?

T: I'm trying to understand. Was it different in the past?

K: Yes, of course it was different.

T: What was different?

K: There was more going on. We went out, we hung out with friends, we had fun or we took a trip with the children, we went to the mountains or something like that, we don't do anything like that anymore.

T: Why not?

K: I don't know, no special reason. Now that I think about it, I believe we have even more time than years before. The house is done, our daughters are more and more independent, financially we're doing well, maybe the problem is that we're a little older and we aren't up for it anymore.

T: But you want to bring more activities into your daily routine?

K: Yes, something I'd be passionate about.

T: In your relationship with Tanja?

K: Yes, I didn't forget about her. We often talked about going together to a dance class, we share that desire, but we have never really realized it.

T: Yes, the need for fun, studying and experiencing something new is a basic psychic need. How much would you say you have fun in your life?

K: Very little. Sometimes we go out with friends, but I don't enjoy it very much.

T: Do you see dancing as something that would bring Tanja and yourself closer and would give you pleasure?

K: I think I do, but I won't know until I try it.

T: Do you think that perhaps now is time to realize your desires?

K: Maybe it's the right time, I'm still up for it, but I'd like to talk to Tanja.

In order for the client to realize his intention, to talk with his partner, I stopped at this point and helped him with some questions to concretize his plan and increase the possibility to really start with an activity that would help him establish a more satisfying relationship with his partner.

T: You said that you always just talked about your desires. How do you intend to proceed talking about it in order for you to be as successful as you can?

K: I was thinking about checking with her first whether she was still up for it. I don't know why she wouldn't be, but I'd like to ask her again.

T: If we assume that she'll agree with your suggestion, what would be your next move?

K: The next move? I would probably have to take the initiative in order to really realize it.

T: Are you ready for that?

K: Of course I am. I don't think it would take any excessive effort or anything like that from me in order to do so. I know that a friend goes to a dance class with his wife and I could ask him if there's any possibility of joining them.

T: What if this possibility isn't available? Maybe they have been learning for some time now.

K: For some time, yes. I could look on the internet to see whether there are any classes in the city. I think that would be a better solution, I'd prefer for us to be alone.

T: For what reason?

K: Because otherwise we'd spend more time hanging out with others.

T: I thought that maybe the reason is to avoid contact with others.

K: No, I didn't think about it.

T: Alright. When could you present your ideas to your partner?

K: I think I could do that immediately, today after therapy.

T: Next time, could we talk about what you manage to realize regarding the classes?

K: Yes, I hope it'll be a successful discussion.

T: I hope everything goes according to your plans.

K: Thank you.

The client did not link his problems with the dissatisfaction he felt in his relationship. Even if he had not mentioned the desire for intimacy with another woman, I still connected his problems, regarding the beliefs of the choice theory, to a dissatisfying relationship. Of course, his thought about "cheating" shows that his relationship with his wife is not well, even if he describes his marriage as "good". This is why I focused on the needs that are not being appeased in this relationship, at least not enough and not in a satisfying manner. It seems that the routine the client feels is well intertwined in their relationship and it is not limited only to their sexual life, which the client also pointed out.

The decision about establishing new intimate relationships belongs to the client, as also taking responsibility and facing the consequences. Therefore, I did not think I should dwell on it more than I presented in the discussion. The client clearly expressed the desire for a better relationship and his willingness to participate in activities in order to achieve a stronger and happier marriage. That is why further on we focused on choosing connecting behaviours in the relationship with his wife and on a successful appeasement of the needs of them both (to a possible extent, regarding the fact that the client was coming to therapy alone), because discords in a marriage mean that the balance between the needs of both spouses has crumbled.

Up to this point, the client had already learned about some parts of choice theory, with which he places himself more and more in the role of a subject, helping him regain control over his life. He has also read Glasser's book *Staying Together*. Afterwards, he talked with his wife about the intensity of their needs, presenting to each other their quality worlds, which brought them closer. As Alen expressed in therapy, they realized that they both become very coordinated with other needs, and that his need for sexuality is more expressed than his wife's.

We started to talk about the possibility for his wife to join in during therapy in later sessions. I think it would be a good and reasonable decision for their marriage.

Alen's advantage is surely the fact that his wife does not use controlling forms of behaviour in their relationship. She does not reproach him for using erotic material, she does not threaten him (for example, to leave him), she does not extort (also with a possible treatment), punish, blame him, and according to Alen's words, she does not even complain. But it is necessary to consider the fact that she also has problems that could be connected to the dissatisfaction she feels with an important relationship.

It also seems that Alen used controlling behaviours in his relationships with his loved ones and that often made him feel bad. He tries to make his family take him more into consideration by using anger. He has realized that this influences the alienation from his daughters, so we worked on developing some connecting behaviours with them (common activities – running, interests – a phone call to the daughter during the week when she studies in another town, which he has never done until now, etc.)

I never talked with the client about sexuality, as the main problem which brought him here seeking help. I chose this approach because I believed that it would strengthen his image of sexuality in his quality world. I'm sure he keeps these images in his personal world, since they bring him pleasure (there an alcoholic keeps alcohol, a junkie his drugs, a hazarder his games, etc.), this is why I did not have the intention to preserve his obsession with this kind of discussion. The client came to therapy with the intention of ceasing his use of unsatisfying behaviours.

The client performed a self-evaluation about his successes in relationships with people and how to lead a life with more control. In his basic belief, choice theory follows a person and his needs, even in the sense that everyone has his own way of solving problems and that the period of this solving is not limited. This is why I did not pressure the client, I let him determine his own tempo in the process of solving problems and go to the point he was ready to reach. He did not refer in therapy, nor did I ask him, how frequently he still uses virtual erotica, he just kept saying that he has things under control, which made me understand that he did not need it anymore and that he had developed more satisfying ways of appeasing his needs.

The client's improvement was visible through choice theory language too. He stopped using the words "it's happening to me" and started placing himself in an active role and moreover, he stared to recognize the possibilities of choice. The client understands and accepts that things are not happening independently of him, but with the possibility of choosing, he can build his everyday life, giving him control over his life. He understands his behaviours as his own (intentional) choice. From this point of view, I imagine his future to be very optimistic.

Presently, I meet with the client once a month. He is accepting and introducing into his life new important decisions and activities (changing job, enrolling in a high school programme 3+2). I see our therapist-client relationship as a satisfying personal relationship that enables a safe and encouraging atmosphere for studying choice theory and introducing changes into his everyday life.

Problems while growing up

This case study presents a new example of bringing up a child while exerting excessive control and the influence of conjugal problems on a child's problems while growing up. The therapeutic work with the family in the presented example actually means working with the couple and parallel individual therapeutic work with an adolescent with problems while growing up. Before the group meeting phase, the adolescent left the therapeutic process, so there was no family treatment of the case.

Two parents came to a meeting because they were worried about their seventeen-year-old son. They described their son with a great measure of criticism and judgment, because he "still cannot find himself". They answered the question about their son's good qualities by saying that "he definitely has potential, but he does not realize it". During the conversation, they focused on those "potentials", they talked about a promising basketball career in his elementary school years, and about his interests in movies, which was excessive in their opinion. They believed that in the past their son was a "cinephile", but they had "successfully saved him" from this obsession.

From the introductory discussion it is possible to understand that the behaviour of their son Miha has been deviating for some time now, especially since he started high school, or when he entered his adolescent years, from the (ideal) image that they have in their "parenting" quality world. It seems that the parents, especially the mother, are very frustrated because of the situation in school. In their opinion, Miha should have entered the general high school and then continued his studies at one of the natural sciences' faculties. Miha's school grades were high enough to enrol in a graphic design school, where he had problems while entering the fourth grade. According to his parents, Miha does not show any interest in school, he also skips classes frequently. He spends little time at home, and he hangs out with his friends a lot in the evenings. His parents suspect that he smokes "something else" besides cigarettes and that he often gets drunk. They are worried about their son and his future.

The "material" that Miha's parents brought to the meeting within the context of the theory of "illness" shows that Miha is trying to reduce his frustration, using the chosen behaviours, but he has not found a behaviour that is effective enough in order to appease his needs and that is acceptable to him and his parents. When Miha comes for a session, we will talk about learning how to effectively appease his current needs and re-establish a satisfying relationship with his parents and other people. The parents wanted first to come alone, to present their son's problems, but I intend to invite them to the counselling process as well, since I believe that their son's behavioural problems are connected to their conjugal problems.

T: I think you have told me a lot about your son. What do you expect from me, according to what you told me?

F (father): We'd like you to take our son for a consultation.

T: I am, of course, willing to talk with Miha. I'm interested in your expectations.

F: I think that my wife and I have done everything we could. We'd do anything for Miha, he's our only child, but at the moment I don't know what else we could do. We're not a match for this situation, Miha needs a professional who would help him from this mess. I think he's deep into it.

T: Maybe this seems a little harsh, but there's no magic wand that would turn your son into you want him to be. The expectations that a professional can "fix" something that has been happening for years are excessive. Besides that, a person can only change his life for the better by himself, with the help of a therapist, of course. However, without the child's and the parents' collaboration, I cannot make changes for the better. I think it's important that we separate this responsibility from the start. Are you ready for that kind of collaboration? This means that you would be actively involved in the therapeutic process as well, that you would participate in the changes which your son would try to introduce into his life.

M (mother): I want to participate as much as I can. Miha is the most important person in my life.

F: I'm also ready to participate, if Miha plays a fair game and doesn't do these stupid things behind our backs.

T: The three of us, we do have a certain influence on what Miha will do, but this doesn't mean that he will actually behave as we want him to. He's still the one who decides what kind of behaviours he'll adopt in the future and he'll be the one responsible for it. My work with Miha, depending of course on how much he wants it, will focus on better choices — on learning how to appease his needs in a more successful way, that is not so threatening to him, and that you would find acceptable as well. The behaviours you use in your relationship with Miha are just as important. They help you build a better relationship and feel more satisfied. During our sessions, we could talk about how you could individually, and together, as a couple, choose new behaviours in your relationship with Miha, and also with each other. What do you think?

M: When you were talking about relationships, I was thinking that I haven't felt close to Miha for a long time. As if I don't know my own child anymore. He has changed so much. As a mother, I can see that he's unhappy, that despite everything he is very lonely and I feel bad for him. It also makes me sad that he sees us as enemies when all we do is meant well since we're his parents!

T: This means that you want to connect more with your son, to be close to him, as you said?

M: Yes, that would mean a lot to me. I want him to know that I still love him and that he can talk to me about his problems.

T: That's what you want. What are your thoughts, Sir?

F: Of course, I want us to be more like a family, and not as we are now, but I think that my wife and I, we have already tried everything!

T: If you want, we can take a look at other existing possibilities together. I have in mind mostly new choices regarding choosing various behaviours, as I mentioned before.

F: I don't know what exactly is expected from me, but I'm willing to talk, of course.

T: That's good; however, in order to improve the relationship, you will have to make some changes. We could become aware of them during our sessions. Are you ready for that?

F: I'm ready to find out what more I can do.

T: We've been talking for an hour and a half. I suggest we continue our session next week. Do you agree that we finish for today and to meet again next week?

F and M: We agree.

F: Could we meet next week, same day, same time?

T: Agreed.

During the next session with Miha's patents I intend to get to know their quality world and not just the ideas and wishes they have regarding Miha, but about themselves as well – in their roles of mother, father, partner – and their marriage. I would like to assess the "condition" of their marriage. I think that they use controlling behaviours in the relationship with their son as well as in their relationship with each other. Regarding the objective that they want to attain, I will focus on their actual behaviour in their relationship with Miha and in their own relationship. I will orient them towards a self-evaluation of these behaviours in terms of how successful they actually are, how efficient they are, and for them to find new possibilities together.

T: During our first session, you said that you have already tried numerous approaches to feel better at home. What exactly did you have in mind?

F: As I said the last time, the problems started at the end of elementary school. We stopped him from going to basketball practice because of his bad grades, regardless of the fact that Miha was very fond of this sport. But we didn't yield and made him leave the club.

T: I don't understand the purpose of this.

F: We wanted him to do better at school.

T: OK, I understand that you made this decision because you wanted to help your son and you believed that it would help, even though you used an ineffective behaviour. I'd like to know how Miha reacted to your decision.

F: I think that that was the turning point. It gave birth to all of his shenanigans.

T: How did they manifest themselves?

F: In the form of defiance, disobedience, leaving home, resisting everything we said.

M: I remember that at the time the situation home was very bad. We pushed him, tried different approaches to make him listen to us, but Miha just got more and more crazy.

F: I think that at the time we started taking tranquilizers.

M: Some time later, maybe after a year. I have been taking antidepressants for two years now.

T: As I understand it, you realized that your decision hadn't turned out the way you wanted, meaning that Miha didn't start to work harder in school. Actually, the opposite; you realized that you had become even more distant and that this decision affected you too. Now, if you take a look back, do you have any idea how you could have behaved so everyone would have suffered less?

M: I don't know what to say. What my husband said is true. The more we tried, the more Miha went out, and the discord at home just kept increasing.

T: I understand that Miha's reaction to your behaviour surprises you, but in theory we know that children's needs change when they reach puberty – their need for power, assertion, freedom increase, and the need for belonging, especially to parents, is marginalized. A lot of parents react the same way you did and a lot of them continue this behaviour even when they realize that it doesn't work. It's great that you decided to talk when you realized that your way wasn't working. However, a lot of adolescents, and also adults, would react the same way Miha did, because we're all sensible to punishments, threats … and that doesn't help to maintain a good relationship in any way. Something very important was taken away from Miha. I'm thinking about basketball. I think it was this activity that helped him successfully satisfy his psychic needs. Since you said that he loved basketball, I believe he was very good at it.

F: He had potential, that's what his coach told me.

T: This activity helped Miha experience what we all need – the feeling of being, being successful, important, free, of having fun, he had the possibility to be creative, and besides all that it was a team sport, so he was able to make friends, develop a sense of belonging. Miha's current behaviour, as you described it, shows that he isn't successfully appeasing these needs; moreover, he is trying to appease them in ways that are harmful and non-acceptable for you, otherwise you wouldn't be here. But I'll talk directly with Miha regarding the possibilities to find better choices for him, and we could talk about your choices of how to behave in your relationship with Miha. What do you think?

F: I don't know exactly what choices you have in mind, but I understand that not letting him play basketball was a bad choice.

T: I believe that you made this decision believing that it would help, that it would change your son's behaviour. I also believe that after that, Miha started to rebel even more, because of his attempts to maintain or to regain power, freedom and everything else I mentioned before. At the same time, I think that he let you know clearly enough that you cannot change him. I'm sure that by choosing these extremely controlling behaviours, you and your son influenced your mutual misunderstanding of one another.

M: Earlier, when you asked me about the situation at home, the first thing I remembered was all the shouting. We shout a lot, all three of us. Maybe we're all trying to enforce our opinions. Speaking of control, Miha experiences it. We tried to control his every step, but it wasn't possible. Even when we tried to limit his curfew he didn't stick to it. He doesn't obey us!

T: Let's go back to your behaviour, since we said that it's not possible to change Miha's or anyone else's behaviour.

M: Yes, OK. I just wanted to say that my husband and I, we were very hard on him. But it didn't help. We achieved the opposite, as we're realizing now.

T: Yes, we're talking about that. Coercion, threatening, extorting, buying off, punishing … as parents we use them all when we feel frustrated, when our child doesn't not behave as we want him to, so we use these behaviours in order to control the relationships we have with our loved ones. I remember you saying that you don't feel connected to your son anymore.

M: It's true. I have no idea what the reason could be, but Miha also contributed to the whole situation, it wasn't just me and my husband.

T: It's not my intention to make you feel guilty. The fact is that you're starting to realize that the situation at home isn't good and you want to change it. But before doing that, it's best to do some self-evaluation about the behaviours you use now, and whether they are effective or not. Miha is using his current choices to regain some control over his life, but unsuccessfully, there's no doubt about it and I'll try to work with him on that.

M: I believe what you're saying, I can see some truth in it. But at the moment I'm very angry at Miha and I find it difficult to accept that my husband and I are responsible for his stupid behaviour.

T: Do you think that you two, as parents, can be responsible for Miha's actions? Can you change his behaviour?

M: No, that's not it.

T: What I believe is that by using the behaviours we talked about earlier we destroy our relationships. And good relationships are necessary for appeasing psychic needs. Through these relationships we can appease our needs. That's why it would be good to work on improving your mutual relationships. When I talk about relationships I also have in mind your marriage. How do you see your marriage, how satisfying is it for you?

F: I don't know what our marriage could have to do with Miha's problems?!

T: We're talking about good relationships with which we appease our needs, which also makes us feel good. And marriage is a very important relationship. I also believe that eventual marital problems can be connected to a child's problems, an adolescent's problems, especially because of the use of controlling behaviours. This is why I'm asking how satisfying your marriage is in your eyes.

F: Our marriage is this ... we consensually decided to stay together. We function as average partners, we have a quiet understanding with which we both agree.

M: It's no secret ... I think ... in a sort of way, we don't talk about it with friends, but we trust you, and I can calmly tell you that my husband has been having an affair with another woman for several years and I don't oppose it. We discussed it, we agree on it, and we don't talk about it anymore.

I have some difficulty believing that the wife does not feel frustrated in her marriage. It is difficult to imagine any woman, whose image of her marriage in her quality world would represent her partner having a relationship with another woman. In this context, I imagine that she is appeasing one of her needs, maybe an existential one, but on a psychic level — I believe it is about the need for power in the sense of concern, control, and dependency of her husband on her — she feels like a "cheated" wife. Regardless of the type of the need, I'm sure that they are both appeasing at least one need in this relationship and that is why they are maintaining their marriage. Consequently, I did not continue to pose questions regarding their satisfaction with their marriage.

T: Do you want to make any changes in the relationship with your husband?

M: No, I don't want to talk about our marriage. We're here because of Miha.

T: What do you want regarding the relationship with your wife?

F: I want it to remain as it is. I agree that we should talk about Miha, I want to participate fully, but I also want the relationship between me and my wife to remain as it is.

T: OK, I respect your decision. You wanted me to talk to Miha, that's why I'm inviting you to keep coming back for more sessions. It would be good to regularly examine the effectiveness of the new behaviours, the satisfaction with the relationship ... what do you think?

M: These sessions are good for me. I'd like to come back.

F: Me too. I agree to meet on a regular basis.

By asking them about their marriage and with the hypothesis of their conjugal problems influencing their child's problems, I risked that they would feel offended and that they would cease coming to the sessions, by which they would lose the possibility of improving their son's life. Nevertheless, they still want to continue with our sessions, which means that they have realized that our meetings are good for them. However, they "overlooked" the fact that Miha's problems are connected to their controlling behaviours, which destroyed their marriage as well. In spite of the visible symptomatic of a dissatisfying marriage (taking antidepressants, extra conjugal relationships, etc.) they did not want to work on improving their relationship, although I believe that if they successfully change their controlling behaviours, it will reflect on and improve all of their relationships.

The two of them cannot picture having a more satisfying role in their partnership, but they do not want to abandon their role of parents, in fact they want to have a better relationship with their son, which I find to be very important for Miha and their mental health. In their relationship with the child, which took the form of a "pathologic" triangle (victim-persecutor-saviour), they had a concordant approach, and we never faced a possible discordant regarding the educational approach.

Miha's parents have been coming regularly to our sessions for some months and at the same time I have been having sessions with Miha. They had some difficulties giving up behaviours of external control psychology despite realizing that the "house detention" they used in the past "does not work anymore", that it lost its power, and had a damaging influence on their relationships. With the help of these meetings, they are realizing that their relationship with their son is more important than some successes, and that precisely through this relationship, when connecting with their son, they can do more. A minimal communication and connection with his parents enhance the possibilities of Miha starting to do his school work and giving up damaging behaviours. This is why we moved from Miha's problematic to a form of behaviour that would help them get closer to their son – what they can do to improve their relationship with him.

In the following extract I expose a part of their learning process about choice theory from the conversation we had about Miha when he made an important decision for himself, although it differed from the images in his parents' quality world regarding his future. Despite the fact that his parents had learned about choice theory and the importance of good relationships, their first and basic belief about their son's news still originated from external control psychology.

F: You know, two days ago, our son really shocked us. We went together to a basketball game, like we discussed here, and we had a great time. Then he went out with his friends and later that day he presented us with his latest news. I thought he was high but he looked very serious, almost like an adult, as he explained that he wants to move to another country.

T: What happened then?

F: My wife panicked and started yelling and waving her arms around, then pleading with him …

T: What about you?

F: I became the old Marko again, I started yelling that he had finally lost his mind, what on earth was he smoking and what else would he do to get on our nerves.

T: What did you want to achieve with that?

F: To stop him before he made the biggest mistake of his life.

T: In six months Miha will be an adult. What will you do then?

F: I know that I can't actually prevent him from living his life. But I never expected something like that! And then he continued to develop his idea of going to Australia, to a ranch, after finishing the third year of high school or in six months or so. My God!

T: So, he intends to finish this year?

F: Yes, he wants to finish the school year, it now seems.

T: I think it's great news.

F: It is. We're happy about it. But the ranch, I think …

T: What is the problem, the ranch or going abroad?

F: Both.

M: Yes, both.

T: I'm not so sure that I understand what it is that you find so unacceptable. Young people have been searching for better opportunities abroad for quite some time now.

F: That's true, but with a degree in his pocket and not without even finishing high school. It's difficult to find a good job abroad.

T: Despite what you think, is there a possibility for you to express some interest in his idea, maybe support him in this plan?

M: I understand that this is how we should have acted then, but at the time I really couldn't bring myself to do it.

T: Perhaps during your next discussion you could focus on your relationship?

M: I could ask him more about his plan, because it didn't seem very concrete, but I still don't agree with his idea.

T: I assume Miha didn't ask you for your permission to go.

M: Of course not, he just presented the idea with confidence, without any doubts about it.

T: Do you remember when we talked about attempts at control and the fact that they just increase the rebellion?

F: Yes. So, is there a greater chance of him doing that if we try to prevent him from going?

T: Maybe. I'm wondering whether Miha just needs more freedom and he's going to search for it abroad, or he's just trying to control you – what more he can do and still have you two accepting, loving him.

F: I had the feeling that he was just testing our self-control as well.

M: What should we do?

T: Yes, what can you do without jeopardizing the relationship with him? You worked hard just to start talking with him again and I think you don't want to lose that.

M: Of course not. We could talk more calmly, tell him that we worry about him, that we want him to finish his studies first and then decide on his future. Maybe also tell him we know that we can't prevent him from carrying out his plan. Like we have discussed so far.

T: Yes, I think it's very good. To explain to Miha what your thoughts are, that behind all the yelling, blaming and threats lies your distress, your worry about how he'll get around in a foreign country, his unfinished studies, insufficient knowledge of a foreign language …

F: I think we'll make him powerless. He expected us to get angry and try to prevent him from going. I think that our acceptance would completely surprise him.

T: It could happen. However, you also have to bear in mind that he may carry out his plan. What then in this case? Could you accept that?

F: Maybe it's not so bad for him to experience being alone in a foreign country. He may start to appreciate more what he has at home.

T: He'll definitely have to take responsibility for his decision.

M: Yes, I think our reaction was too choleric. It depends on how serious he really is. Well, maybe he'll tell you about his plans too.

We slowly concluded the meeting. I could have found out more, what kind of future they want for their son, how they could support him in his ideas, which obviously became more creative, etc. But Miha's idea did not bring anything concrete, so I suppose that it was really an attempt to regain power, a message for his parents, that he will create his future according to his ideas.

During the therapeutic process, Miha's parents were presented with the choice and behaviour theory that could help them substitute external control psychology, which has been destroying their marriage and the family's happiness for some years. Regardless of Miha's behaviour, they try to express support, acceptance, and love, encourage him, help him, negotiate with him, etc., everything they were doing in the past, before becoming "yellers", who have mistakenly believed that with coercion and punishments they could change one another. They are learning and getting to know, step by step, the freedom that choice theory brings them.

Miha also came to a session. He tried to establish control over me and himself with an inaccessible pose and a scornful expression. His body language let me know that he believed he was there because "others wanted that". He believed himself to be an involuntary client who has no choice and does only what others order him to do. Therefore, my first task was to establish a relationship which would not include interrogation, blaming, slamming, and other destructive behaviours, and would help Miha realize that he came to the meeting for himself. Without this realization, I do not believe that Miha would come back in the future.

The precondition to reach successful results, I realize, is that Miha is not affected by controlling behaviours, as he was at home, and certainly within the educational system, when he had to "go and have a talk". I have to make sure that he feels good during our session so, as stated by choice theory, he will be able to appease his needs with success. According to the meetings I had with his parents, I believe that it would be a good idea to make Miha feel some belonging, acceptance, and also respect.

T: Hello. Is it OK if we are on a first name basis?

K: Yes, no problem.

T: Was it difficult to get here?

K: Not really. I know this part if the town and I didn't have any problems. Also, my parents told me where you are.

T: What were you thinking on your way here? What were your thoughts?

K: Ha ha. I was thinking, yes. That I want it to be over soon.

T: Anything else maybe?

K: When would theystop taking me around, to professionals!

T: I don't see the two of them getting you here. Didn't you come alone?

K: Ha ha. I come alone, but they sent me.

T: You could have chosen not to come.

K: I could have not come, but I don't feel like listening to their lectures, that's why I'm here.

T: If I understand, you had to choose between not coming here and listening to your parents' lecture, and coming here?

K: Something like that, yes.

T: Perhaps for starters we could talk about expectations, mine and yours, regarding our sessions. I wanted to tell you that ... as you know, your parents have been coming here for sessions. I would like to assure you that everything we will talk about will stay here, between us. I will tell your parents only about things that could endanger your life. In this case, I'm obliged to do that. For anything else that I'd like to tell your parents, I'll ask your permission first, or I'll advise you to talk to them. Is that OK with you?

K: It seems fair. But it wouldn't bother me if you told them something. But I was also asking myself, on my way here, before when you asked me ... I'd like to know what my parents said about me.

T: Your parents presented the situation at home, as they see and feel it. They also described your behaviours, but we focused our discussion on them and their behaviours, because they expressed the desire to get along with you more.

K: I noticed that they have made more of an effort with me. They seem ridiculous. The other day I asked them where had they been until now! Did they really have to come here to be able to see me?! My father never had time for me, other people have always been more important to him, work was also more important. My mother made sure that everything at home was nice. I remember that she always read to me in the evenings, when I was in elementary school she studied with me. But she mainly followed dad.

T: There is still a possibility for you all to get along together.

K: Maybe. But what do they think …

T: What worries you about their opinion?

K: Nothing worries me, but they have their truth and I have mine.

T: You'll have the opportunity to present how you see and experience these situations. Do you want that?

K: I can also tell you something about them. Everything about me bothers them – how I dress, talk, my friends, the kind of music I listen to, and let's not even mention school.

T: We're not here to talk about each other. It's not about that. We won't talk about your parents, but about you, how you see yourself, experience things, whether you are satisfied with yourself, with your behaviour, with the relationships that are important to you … I think these questions are important for our sessions. But I still don't know what you expect from our meetings, except that they will end as soon as possible (laugh).

K: (laugh) I don't have any expectations. I haven't thought about it. All that was more of an obligation than a desire to work on myself.

T: So, for our next session, could you think about what you want for yourself, what you want to change, what you want to work on, whether you are still willing to come to meetings, of course.

K: I could come. I'll think about something I'd like to talk about.

T: OK. If you aren't able to come, or you don't want to come, please tell me in advance.

K: OK.

I purposely ended our conversation regarding his next visit in a concise and maybe a slightly casual way – I did not let him control me and he got the message that he alone decides about coming to sessions and that he is the only one responsible for his decision. I also gave him time to think about the things he was not ready for.

In our introductory session, through which we mostly tried to establish a connection, as presented here, Miha started thinking about himself, his desires, and needs. Until now his thoughts have been focused on his parents and their expectations and desires in the relationship with him. This is why he came to me. This is the client's explanation, positioning himself in the role of victim, who has no influence on his life and he avoids the responsibility for his own actions. Miha will be confronted with that during the discussion about his current behaviour.

Even if he hadn't expressed the desire to tell his story, I had no intention of including what his parents had told me about him in our session. I want to get to know Miha's quality world, his desires and needs, and the current behaviours he uses to attain his personal goals and orient him towards a self-evaluation of the efficacy of these behaviours.

…

T: Miha, for today we agreed to talk about your desires and needs, about the goals you want to reach.

K: I thought a little about this, yes. Talking about school, high school, I know I'll finish it, because I want to.

T: How about skipping the classes?

K: I skip just the number of classes I know I can. I study just enough to pass the school year.

T: It seems that you have enough control over that matter. How satisfied are you with the final result?

K: I'm satisfied, I don't need more.

T: Enough for what? What plans do you have? How do you see your professional career?

K: For me, high school is enough, I don't need more. The two of them can have their faculties … I'd like to work with computers, graphic design. That's it. I don't have any problems with that, they do because they think that I have to be something extra and super, like their friends' children. I'm completely satisfied with my current achievements. To me freedom is more important than success.

This is the source of the conflicts in Miha's family – the appeasing of Miha's exceptional need for freedom and power and his parents' exceptional need for power and importance. I believe the key question in order for them all to understand each other is how Miha would keep or regain his freedom and his parents the importance, while maintaining a good relationship.

T: How do you imagine freedom in your relationship?

K: That they'd let me breathe, accept me, and that I wouldn't have to constantly listen to them, about what, how … I should behave.

T: You're thinking about your parents?

K: Them, yes.

T: Does this bad relationship help you achieve your desired freedom?

K: They bother me for a while, then they give up and finally I have peace.

T: How do you feel at home?

K: Miserable, but I have become used to it, it's been like that for a few years now.

T: Do you want to get along with your parents?

K: Why can't they accept me as I am?! What's wrong with me?! Am I not good enough for them?!

T: I think you're a nice boy, I don't know why there should be anything wrong with you. Everyone has different ideas of how someone else should behave, what should he do with his life. We do that especially to people that we love, who are important to us. It seems that your parents have some defined ideas about you and your future. When there's such deviation, you have to talk, to make compromises that are acceptable to both sides. Are you ready to negotiate with them in order to gain your freedom?

K: What would that look like?

T: As you say, you gain your freedom by getting into a conflict with them, but afterwards you feel bad at home. Could you get your freedom in another way – one that would make you keep a good relationship with them? Do you want that?

K: The situation at home seems much more complicated to me.

T: Do you have something particular in mind?

K: Yes, I don't know how honest my parents have been, because they behave like no one alive knows, but usually everyone does know. Well, in our case the wife also knows. And you wouldn't believe it, my mother puts up with it calmly.

T: Are you thinking about your father's relationship with another woman?

K: Oh, they've told you. It's a pretty big thing, isn't it?!

T: It's their decision. I understand that, despite that, they're still satisfied with their marriage. They know what it is that keeps the marriage alive. I'd like to ask you how important this situation within their relationship is for you. How does it influence the relationship you have with them, or you personally?

K: His behaviour bothers me. It's a little easier because I know my mother is OK, as well as she could be. But his behaviour really bothers me. In the past, when we occasionally went to see a game together, I felt some warmth between us at odd moments, but in the same instant I realized that he really was a pig for doing that to my mum.

T: I believe that he's doing that for him and not to hurt your mother. But it probably is, no matter how we look at it, painful for all of you. Children often feel guilty for what's happening to their parents' marriage, which is, of course, completely unjustifiable. A marriage is the adults' responsibility, not the children's. Do you feel guilty sometimes? You seem angry.

K: I'm angry at him. I never actually said that it may be partly my fault, but maybe subconsciously I feel sort of a guilt. They sometimes used to have fights because of me, but now they seem more unified.

T: Why do you think that is so?

K: Maybe they're worried about me.

T: It's normal that a child with "problematic" behaviour gains the parents' attention. The parents start to focus actively together on him. This also tells you that you mean a lot to them. Even today. Would you like to talk to them about their relationship? What would it mean to you? Would you feel better?

K: I don't know. The current situation at home is too difficult.

T: Perhaps that could be an opportunity to get closer and realize that you could get along even though the choices that aren't optimal for all.

K: I'll see. I have to think about it and decide whether I even want to deal with that.

T: OK. Decide in accordance with the way to better your relationship with them. If we go back to your freedom ... are you prepared to achieve it in another way?

K: I don't know, I don't have a real idea of what I could do differently. I am speaking to them currently. I didn't for some time in the past, because we always ended up discussing the same old *stories about school, and the only way I could get any peace was to stay silent, to not communicate with them.*

[...]

Miha is exerting a form of control over his parents by rebelling and not listening, but also by ignoring them, not giving them any attention or not communicating with them. This harsh behaviour towards them is not a solution for the loss of freedom and acceptance. I will focus the conversation with Miha on searching for less painful ways of appeasing his needs, especially the need for freedom.

[...]

T: How do you see yourself in this relationship? Who's responsible for the relationship?

K: I think all of us are, but I don't know whether I have any need for this.

T: It depends on what you want. If you don't want to remain in this relationship, or you don't have any intention of improving it, no one can force you to do so. You decide what kind of relationships you'll have with other people. But your satisfaction depends on that. We can appease our psychic needs only through the relationships we have with other people. You mentioned your need for freedom, belonging, acceptance, consideration, respect ...

K: I don't know what to say. Hanging out with my friends means a lot to me.

T: I believe you. You are in a phase where you find it easier to appease the needs I mentioned before through the relationships you have with your friends, because you all have similar aspirations. You parents want something else for you, and for you not to skip school and stay out with your friends. I think it's normal that your friends are important to you, and these good relationships with them must mean a lot to you ...

K: They do, yes. Especially because there's no yelling and no one is telling me what to do. We listen to music, we talk, we feel good.

Miha is trying to get some satisfaction through social activities which include other people and demand from him the ability to maintain good relationships. I think this is good – he is not lonely and miserable, he is appeasing his needs through the relationships with his peers. He may have withheld some activities but I did not want to press further, because it would seem like an interrogation, which would not help. I continued by evaluating the relationships at home and searching for better choices. If Miha does not realize the importance of good relationships and his role in them – regardless of his parents' behaviour – there will not be any change.

T: Yes. The situation at home probably hasn't always been the same as today. What was it like when you still felt good at home?

K: The images I have are a little faded. I always told them everything, they wanted to know everything. The best memories I have are about the basketball matches. They always came to watch and cheer for me, and afterwards we went out for pizza.

T: What are the behaviours you used at the time that helped you get closer to your parents? Or maybe even better, what types of behaviour in your friendships help you today to maintain good relationships?

K: It's different with friends, more carefree. Whatever I say is OK. But with them … When I was younger they could buy me with anything. Now things are different.

T: We're talking about the relationship, the behaviours that could help you get close again. What would it mean to you to get along with them again?

K: Maybe I'd be calmer inside or more satisfied with myself.

T: What can you do now to achieve peace and satisfaction?

K: I don't know if I'm even ready to do anything, I'm not sure that I even want to be closer to them.

T: You say that you don't feel good at home.

K: I don't.

T: And you want to feel more peaceful, satisfied. Are you willing to change anything?

K: What could I do?

T: You mean, how could you get closer with your parents?

K: I don't like that idea too much.

T: Could you obtain what you want in any other way?

K: I think I'm not ready. I don't feel like working on that.

T: What are you willing to work on? What do you think is important?

K: Only that I leave the house as soon as possible.

I dare say that Miha's family has been divided by the criticism they used to change one another, to try to control their lives. This explicitly destructive behaviour has brought them only division and alienation.

Actually, Miha cares a lot about school. He intends to finish the school year and so far he has never had to repeat a year. This calculation is also Miha's form of exerting control over his parents. He knows exactly how much his school achievements mean to them, and that his attitude towards school bothers and worries them. He appeases his need for power and freedom by leaving them in the dark about his school grades until the last moment. But Miha believes in himself, in his capacities, and his potential to be successful (enough) in school.

Miha's parents used control theory for their son's education. They had and still have specific images about their child, and their efforts, or in other words constraints, were focused on him achieving these images. Miha's self-destructive behaviour is his way of expressing the disagreement with his parents' desires – rebelliousness. Miha started to distance himself from his parents; he started appeasing his need for belonging and power with his "gang" and substance abuse. In Glasser's opinion, the behaviours he chose are typical for children with parents who have not taken enough time to discover what their child really wants and to negotiate about these differences when they present themselves.

It is evident that the parents did a lot of things *for him*, for Miha. When they were not willing to do that anymore, they replaced *for him* with *to him* and tried to make Miha a better student through yelling and threats. The control had its price. Miha stopped feeling good in the presence of his parents, their image in his quality world started to fade.

I believe Miha's creative behaviour is connected to the relationship he has with his parents, and that the improvement of this relationship is essential for him being satisfied with his life. This is why I focused on the aspect, which Miha has not yet recognized as important for his well-being. It is true that his parents jeopardized their presence in Miha's quality world by punishing, insulting, and underestimating him. Regardless of the type of behaviour, the parents choose, in their relationship with Miha, to always be present in his quality world and Miha in theirs.

T: Do you want me to invite you parents to our next session and talk all together about your desires for the future?

K: No, I don't want to. I won't be here.

T: Why's that?

K: I was thinking about leaving the house, to get away from them.

T: That's what I understood. Do you intend to talk to them about it?

K: Not here. I'll let them know in due time.

T: Can I help you with that? How have you imagined an independent life?

K: I have thought about it. Soon I'll be eighteen and I'd like to live alone.

T: What would that give you?

K: A feeling of freedom.

T: What are the real possibilities of you living alone? Realistically speaking, when could that happen?

K: Probably not so soon.

T: So, before you move out a lot of time will pass. Do you intend to spend this time not feeling good at home? This could go on for some time.

K: It depends. If they "try harder" at home, the possibilities are good. I don't know whether they would do that. They would probably try to negotiate that over my studies.

T: Would you negotiate that with them?

K: I would. But it depends on how far they're willing to go.

T: How could this calculation influence your relationship with them?

K: Probably not so promisingly.

T: Since we're talking about calculations … I believe that your path towards independence would be much easier if you had a good relationship with your parents.

K: You think?

T: Parents that have good relationships with their children are usually more supportive. How probable do you think it that your parents will help you financially to gain your independence if you aren't willing to do anything to better your relationship?

K: We're talking now, so I could ask them.

T: Aha, a better relationship makes it possible for you to talk about it with them. What is more convenient for you, to take care of your finances all by yourself, or to develop a relationship with them and consequently receive some financial support?

K: I understand what you're trying to tell me. I have to think about it.

[...]

At the end of the session Miha thanked me and expressed the desire not to come to any more sessions. He agreed on the suggestion about leaving the "option" to come again, if he wanted to. We decided that he would be the one informing his parents about the decision.

It is possible to recognise small changes in Miha's behaviour (communication with his parents, willingness to negotiate, learning to accept others' behaviours, thinking about his future, etc.) He is keeping some ineffective and damaging choices, which he is not ready to turn into positive ones. He is using some excuses and one of them may be his father's affair.

In his childhood, Miha did not have enough opportunities to create images that would help him achieve a sense of well-being and create a quality life. He would learn about taking an effective control over his life from his parents if they did more things together, if they substituted *for him* and *to him* with *with him* and by doing that, help him learn about independency and responsibility, which he needs as an adult. The roots of the problem are the parents' exactly defined images about what kind of an adult "their" Miha should become. The parents are now easing up on their images and would be satisfied if Miha just finished graphic design school and stopped harming his health. Nonetheless, the period of a child's education through discipline (not punishments), that would help him to keep some control, is already over. Miha is thinking about an independent life, but he is not equipped for that. This may be the part of his life where he could start taking some responsibilities, start to negotiate, and discuss with his parents. It is his decision.

We did not get the chance to make some plans with Miha. When he reached the point where he would have to do something, make some changes in his life, which demand a more active role on his part, he was not willing to do any of that and he seemingly devalued the whole situation. Perhaps, simply put, Miha is not unhappy enough, maybe he is rebelling just because the "help process" was initiated by his parents and not him. Although Miha is not coming to any more sessions, his parents decided, despite his decision, to continue the sessions with me.

Concluding Conceptualization

The discussed material was full of implicit theories (*'theories in use'* by Schon); they are hidden comprehensions of the clients, comprehensions that the clients do not know or say, but are evident from the viewpoint of the chosen theories legitimacy. The material is working, implicit, which we point out or explain through the client's reflection, or realizations. This is also taken into consideration by the case study, completed by the therapist's internal dialogue (the interpretation of the perceived), which simultaneously explains and makes people aware of the client's behaviour. We realize the risk of the stigmatization effect, which can be caused by the formation of implicit theories, but it is necessary to understand that the psychotherapeutic practice, whose work methods are based on psychotherapeutic theory, also includes pre-determined axioms, which represent important aspects for the therapeutic treatment.

At the saturation point, when the data became repetitive and redundant for further work, it was possible to grasp from the analysis of the material the clients' determined behavioural patterns, which speak in favour of the chosen theory.

Form one:[46] the clients persistently recognize themselves in the roles of victims of other people's actions, they themselves have no power or influence, because they understand their actions and consideration as causal-consecutive.

- *"I'd like to feel equal to her. But I don't know if it's even possible."*

- *"Then why do I have to do everything that he tells me?"*

- *"I wanted that, yes, but I always subordinated to my mother's orders."*

- *"I feel bad because of what I'm doing. I think I need help, but I don't see how could I get rid of that, since it's accessible to me all the time and I don't have the strength to resist it"*

- *"Why can't they accept me as I am?! What's wrong with me?! Am I not good enough for them?!"*

Form two: they consider others guilty for their problems – external factors – close people or past events, which they have no influence on.

- *"She has a plan in her mind, regarding what needs to be done that day and she does not deviate from that, not for a second. When everything is done, she is extremely satisfied, you can really see how satisfied she is. But I am nervous, because there is no time for my things, my brother is also nervous, our father is used to this."*

---

[46] Besides each form, we have put an example as an illustration from each case study – if the behaviour has, of course, been recognized.

- *"His mother was always there, which drives me to even bigger despair"*

- *"They wouldn't let me near them."*

- *"Right now, just as I was listening to you, I could see before my eyes scenes, literally see the scenes, people with whom I don't want to deal anymore. My shoulders would really feel lighter. I think my past is my burden."*

- *"The more we tried, the more Miha went out, and the discord at home just kept increasing."*

Form three: the clients put a lot of energy into attempts to exercise control over others or in withdrawals from others' control. For that they use controlling or other destructive behaviours.

- *"We're allies in the relationship with our mother to a point. She persecutes us both, but we also use each other as an excuse. As an older brother, I believe that I have more rights and I believe that he should listen to me."*

- *"The constant arguing, quarrels, she doesn't even want to eat with me anymore, let alone anything else."*

- *"I hadn't done anything in some time, because there's no communication between us. She said that I'm dead to her, so she's dead to me."*

- *"I remember the fights between my parents, especially when my father came home drunk and yelled at me and my mother. He was often very violent to both of us, especially my mother. Then I went to my room to have some peace, to hide from what was happening. I think that I masturbated in order to comfort myself, as if the pain would lessen. But these fights were quite frequent since my father was an alcoholic, and because of that I masturbated regularly."*

- *"Earlier, when you asked me about the situation at home, the first thing I remembered was all the shouting. We shout a lot, all three of us. Maybe we're all trying to enforce our opinions. Speaking of control, Miha experiences it. We tried to control his every step, but it wasn't possible. Even when we tried to limit his curfew he didn't stick to it. He doesn't obey us!"*

Form four: in their last important relationships all the treated clients experienced constraining and controlling behaviour. In some cases, those actions were 'hidden' behind care, love, good-intentions, etc., especially from the mother's side.

- *"[...] my mother cannot understand that I need time for myself. She wants me to work all day, she is constantly giving me orders."*

- *"You don't want to talk, you want to give orders, so that everything would be as you say. And if I don't agree, there's a fight coming."*

- *"[...] She starts rolling her eyes, or she swings her arm and she tells me to go somewhere, or she replies curtly."*

- *"But it's just now that I feel really free, the last 2 years since my mother's death. Before that, everywhere I went, she was waiting for me at the door. When I was 15 and when I was 40. [...] She was afraid to be alone, so I stayed most of the time confined in the apartment with her. I only ran to the supermarket and back and if it took me more than an hour, she was beside herself."*

- *"On the other hand, she was always very demanding towards me, it was difficult for me to reach her standards, even as a child. She wanted me to be very good in school, but I didn't like studying and because of that I was under pressure. Even today, she still pressures me to get an education, to be successful, important. Now I just tell her to get lost, I don't let her annoy me."*

- *"We pushed him, tried different approaches to make him listen to us ..."*

Form five: as a rule, the clients received an authoritative form of education from the parents. During the therapeutic process, some of them show that distinctively in connection to low self-esteem and low self-confidence.

- *"To me, my mother seems like a cop, her behaviour reminds me of the time I spent in the army, constantly under control and obeying orders. It makes me crazy! No one can stand her dictatorship."*

- *"When I tried to do things my way she always tightened her hold on me (mother – note Podgornik). [...] When he (father – note Podgornik) came home, there had to be total silence otherwise we were punished, even scuffled."*

- *"I remember the fights between my parents, especially when my father came home drunk and yelled at me and my mother. He was often very violent to both of us, especially my mother. [...] I realize that I tried my best, even at home when possible, to be a good and obedient child, so there were no fights, or that my father didn't scream because of me. But I also realize that I'll never be the son she wishes me to be."*

- *"I just wanted to say that my husband and I, we were very hard on him."*

Form six: the destructive effects of actions of external control psychology on personal relationships and on an individual's mental health are evident.

- *"Near my mother I feel like a ten-year-old boy who needs instructions on what he can and can't do, what he has to do in order to make mum happy, without any right to his own opinion."*

- *"It's difficult to get used to it, because we always used to say that we had a headache. I noticed that my head hurts when I'm upset and angry. Now I understand why."*

- *"I'm the type of person that when I get the feeling someone wants to have me only for himself, I end it. I can't stand the feeling of being controlled. I like to be alone and free."*

- *"I think he was a wuss, who couldn't take care of his family. He didn't respect his wife, he was never satisfied with me, I was just a brat in his way. I don't have any good memories, nothing good ties me to my father."*

- *"When you were talking about relationships I was thinking that I haven't felt close to Miha for a long time. As if I don't know my own child anymore. He has changed so much. As a mother, I can see that he's unhappy, that despite everything, he is very lonely and I feel bad for him. It also makes me sad that he sees us as enemies when all we do is meant well since we're his parents!"*

Form seven: the client's intensive concern with symptomatology is present.

- *"My blood pressure went through the roof, I'm so upset that I smoke one cigarette after another even two hours after a fight and I need quite a while to calm down."*

- *"I'm very nervous and I think that I can calm down only when I drink."*

- *"I remember that the day I went to the hospital I went into a library first. I saw a skeleton in front of me again, I heard voices ringing in my head, I didn't know where I was, who I was, I didn't know what the people looking at me were thinking. I had the feeling the ceiling would fall on me, the walls were closing on me and everything was distorted. I remember I couldn't breathe."*

- *"You know, around two years ago, I started stammering in front of others, I just couldn't talk and I had a feeling in my head that I was about to pass out. Very unpleasant. Then I started avoiding others. My wife and I almost stopped hanging out with friends."*

- *"We pushed him, tried different approaches to make him listen to us, but Miha just got more and more crazy."*

Form eight: without exception, in the 'background' of the client's problem there is a momentary unsatisfying and important relationship.

- *"To me, my mother seems like a cop, her behaviour reminds me of the time I spent in the army, constantly under control and obeying orders."*

- *"We realized that we cannot continue this way. We are not getting any younger and our life is getting too difficult."*

- *"Later, our relationship (with the brother – note Podgornik) was more or less severed, because I don't get along with his wife. I see my nephew 5 times a year. My brother comes to see me on his way home from work, but then he hurries home so his wife won't know that he has been visiting me."*

- *"Our relationship is somehow tepid, nothing special, lately I've realized that everything has become just a routine."*

- *"Our marriage is this ... we consensually decided to stay together. [...] We function as average partners, we have a quiet understanding with which we both agree. It's no secret ... I think ... in a sort of way, we don't talk about it with friends, but we trust you, and I can calmly tell you that my husband has been having an affair with another woman for several years and I don't oppose it. We discussed it, we agree on it, and we don't talk about it anymore."*

Form nine: the clients try to appease their psychic needs in ways that are unsatisfying for them or even frustrating and destructive, which they express with somatization and mental suffering.

- *"With anger, screaming, blaming, insulting. I tell her everything. I just explode. I can't stand it anymore."*

- *"To the bar. To play cards and drink."*

- *"Probably some sort of peace, apparent peace – there weren't any conflicts between us, but I felt angry towards her and I had the feeling that I was being wronged."*

- *"I trust you, it's alright. I was thinking, actually I realized that I just fall back to this behaviour when I have a hard time. At that time, there's a force pushing me towards erotica to satisfy myself, get intoxicated and function more easily. At least I thought, I hoped that I would function better, and maybe at the beginning I did, but now it's getting more difficult. Recently, my condition hasn't been good. I think I'm suffering. It's difficult to admit to myself, I'd prefer if it was all just for pleasure and not my nightmare. Except for my work, I don't do anything useful. All the time I think about the next chance to look at those things."*

- *"[...] defiance, disobedience, leaving home, resisting everything we said."*

Form ten: feeling psychically unwell is connected to the client's dysfunctional conviction.

- *"I think she loves books too, it's just that she doesn't read them, so it wouldn't be my way."*

- *"Why should I eat with you when you don't even see me?! You eat with your mother. I, as your wife, don't even exist in that house. Your mother is the important one, not me!"*

- *"There are a lot of them. The fear that I'll go crazy again, the fear of crowds and the dark in a hall, the fear of going into a pool. I wonder how I'll ever go into a pool; what if I fall and am a nuisance to other people."*

- *"I believe I still carry inside of me the sense of inferiority I gained as a child. Even now, after all these years, I can hear my mother telling me that I will accomplish nothing in life. I simply believe that I'm not good enough or not as good as others."*

- *"Yes, I don't know how honest my parents have been, because they behave like no one alive knows, but usually everyone does know. Well, in our case the wife also knows. And you wouldn't believe it, my mother puts up with it calmly."*

Form eleven: the formation of individual dysfunctional convictions is connected to the social construction of sexes, which is a result of an androcentric culture, a patriarchal tradition and sexism.

- *"He (Vid – note Podgornik) had a strong desire to become a priest, but his parents did not approve of this. Even today, when his mother sees him reading books, she tells him angrily to go to a monastery. His mother's mocking hurts him, because it makes him think that what he does is not right, it is not good enough for his parents."*

- *"Now I realize that I have a lot of qualities, that I'm skilled, but in my family that was always questionable, this is why I was laughed at, felt worthless. So, after some years I started to believe that playing the guitar wasn't enough, that reading and painting weren't work. That you are valuable only if you do physical work."*

- *"He never wanted to hear about what I want. I could only take care of the family and work. That yes, but having fun no, God no!"*

- *"I agree but nothing good about what could I do comes to my mind. My wife cooks and the girls help her."*

- *"It's no secret ... I think ... in a sort of way, we don't talk about it with friends, but we trust you, and I can calmly tell you that my husband has been having an affair with another woman for several years and I don't oppose it. We discussed it, we agree on it, and we don't talk about it anymore."*

Form twelve: psychic crises are directly connected to painful experiences and traumatic events, like violence, poverty, disease, personal loss, separation, etc.

- *"After that I fell ill and I had an intestinal operation. The doctor suggested that I work only 4 hours a day. The fact that I wouldn't be able to teach depressed me. What should I do in school for only 4 hours?! School was always the most important thing to me! In the same year, I started to have hallucinations and hear things. This has annihilated me. These facts were followed by my hospitalization and then vegetation from day to day."*

- *"I remember the fights between my parents, especially when my father came home drunk and yelled at me and my mother ... he was often very violent to both of us, especially my mother. [...] But these fights were quite frequent since my father was an alcoholic ..."*

- *"When you were talking about relationships I was thinking that I haven't felt close to Miha for a long time. As if I don't know my own child anymore. He has changed so much. As a mother, I can see that he's unhappy, that despite everything, he is very lonely and I feel bad for him. It also makes me sad that he sees us as enemies when all we do is meant well since we're his parents!"*

Form thirteen: the client's chosen, especially destructive behaviour is connected to sex and social acceptance.

- *"Vid chose a more painful way – depression."*

- *"Ana suffers from severe and frequent headaches and Ivo has a drinking and some somatic problems (he complained a lot because of lower back pain). Both spouses are overweight."*

- *"I started to have hallucinations and hear things." (woman)*

- *"Recently, I read an article about sex addiction and in an instant my eyes opened. That's it. That's happening to me. I'm addicted to sex! Not even to sex, but to erotica."*

- *"It gave birth to all of his shenanigans. [...] defiance, disobedience, leaving home, resisting everything we said."*

- *"I have been taking antidepressants for two years now."*

Form fourteen: the clients have problems with establishing and developing satisfying relationships.

- *"Yes, sometimes I tell her that she could also read, that it wouldn't hurt her. That makes her extremely angry, she becomes furious."*

- *"And what can I do with that power if the next day I'm the one who's subjected to him again?"*

- *"No, I'm not satisfied and I suffer a lot because of that. But I don't want to have anything to do with my sister-in-law, we're too different. The two of them are my only family, but I can't get close to them."*

- "Something like: "Not him. How can I have a conversation with him, I won't be able to manage it. I will feel like fainting, I'll sweat and stammer. He's successful, he acts all superior, and he's inaccessible. What if he asks me what I do in life?"

- "I became again the old Marko again, I started yelling that he had finally lost his mind, what on earth was he smoking and what else would he do to get on our nerves."

Form fifteen: the change in the perception and understanding of our own actions and the actions of others makes it possible for the client to appease his basic psychical needs more effectively and to regain control over his own life.

- "I can see that since I have dedicated more time to guitar playing, concerts, and painting, I feel completely different. I'm satisfied. I have regained the will to live. Before that, nothing I did made any sense to me, because I did everything just to please my mother. I didn't live for myself. I was appeasing her needs, not mine."

- "I started to think that he feels much better in the bar with his friends. That's why he spends there so much time and why he goes there so often. I have never understood what the hell he gets there!"

- "I feel a lot better and my thoughts are not as dark as they used to be. I usually get the feeling that I've never done as much for myself in my life as now."

- "Well, I thought about it last time. The allergies she started to have recently also made me think that they may be connected to our relationship. I think I pressure her too much, that I harass her unnecessarily. You know I thought about the fact that her allergies are merely a consequence of her not expressing her dissatisfaction, last time her face was all swollen."

- "I think we'll make him powerless. He expected us to get angry and try to prevent him from going. I think that our acceptance would completely surprise him."

Form sixteen: the regaining of control over one's life or the amelioration of mental health is directly connected to an effective appeasing of psychical needs in relationships with others.

- "Since I know that work means a lot to her, I ask her frequently if I can help her with something, I also offer to make lunch. She's a very good cook so sometimes she shows me some tricks and I'm happy to learn something new. I often go to the supermarket; I never did that before. I think it's important that I often tried to make her read something, because I really wanted her to, and now that I don't force her anymore, she frequently takes a book and reads it. After that we talk as I always wanted. That makes me happy."

- "And we don't need to work. I don't have that intention. We can enjoy the nature. We could go for a walk, down to the stream, you could pick snowdrops, we could lounge, talk. What do you say?"

- "I've wanted that for a long time, it's true. I think that if I did it again I'd choose to teach English. [...] My brother is a teacher, so he could recommend me. He used to ask me if I'd teach someone, but I always turned him down."

- "Maybe I'd feel better because I'd be doing something for her. I know I feel useful when I visit her and bring her food or anything else she may need. I feel a warmth inside, a nice feeling, which I also have when I do something good for my girls at home."

- "Yes, that would mean a lot to me. I want him to know that I still love him and that he can talk to me about his problems."

As a generalization that has formed on the basis of the analysis of the material and the prepared paradigmatic model, I present the strategy of the client's "behaviour" in the aspect of his "illness" and the strategy of the client's regain of control over his life.

Strategy A: 'The loss of control over one's own life.'

1. *The assuming and/or performing of controlling behaviour.* These clients try unsuccessfully to appease their psychical needs with it, which manifests itself in numerous painful ways (addiction, mental health problems, psychosomatic illness etc.)

2. *Causative-consecutive deliberation and action.* The internalized deliberation that people are beings of reaction, who just react to others' behaviour and do not have any possibility of choice. These clients avoid the realization that they alone, directly or indirectly, chose the very thing they complain about.

3. *The position of the 'nutshell'.* If a person persists in the role of a victim and blames others for his unhappiness and dissatisfaction, his quality of life cannot improve, and neither can his well-being. The client's key realization must be that he can control and also change only his own behaviour and not others.

4. *Persisting in bad, unsatisfying relationships.* People remain for years in unhappy, unconnected relationships, where they try to appease their basic needs in painful ways. They often express their dissatisfaction with complaints and disapproval, but they do not link these unhappy relationships to mental health problems.

5. *Orientation towards a physiological and emotive component of holistic behaviour.* Emotional (sadness, fear, anger, anxiety, etc.) and physical (unrest, pain, general bad state of health, etc.) feelings are the most frustrating and painful for an individual. This is why he focuses himself on them and consequently remains in the magic circle of unhappiness and

suffering. The active component of the holistic behaviour remains practically inactive until entering the therapeutic process.

Strategy B: 'Assuming control over one's own life.'

1. *The orientation towards the client's world of qualities.* A person's internal, personal, and unique world is represented by a group of people, things, events, convictions, values, etc., and it shapes itself from birth, all our life, and it represents the best ways we want to appease our needs. The recognition and taking into consideration of a person's world of qualities are necessary for searching for more effective ways of appeasing needs, which represent the creation of a quality of life and the improvement of health.

2. *The orientation towards choosing more effective behaviours and deliberations.* When a client learns how to remove the external control from his life, he starts to change his actual unsatisfying relationships. Changing the perception and understanding of his own actions and the actions of others enables him a more effective appeasing of his basic psychical needs and regaining of control over his own life. The client's key realization is that he can control and also change only his own actions not the actions of others.

3. *Care for an (equilibrated) appeasing of psychical needs.* Orientation towards appeasing psychical needs by taking into consideration the client's personal world of values, convictions, figures, ideas, etc. A regard for reality and search for solutions, better choices within the given possibilities (environment).

4. *Taking care of relationships and/or establishing new ones.* A person cannot appease all of his psychical needs without a basic consciousness that he is a free being who can choose – a series of behaviours and self-perception and the perception of others –, and that he is a social being who can successfully appease his needs only in a satisfying relationship with other people.

5. *The meaning of the therapist-client relationship.* The therapist-client relationship represents the basis of the whole psychotherapeutic process. We derive from the beliefs of numerous professionals that the meaning of the relation between the therapist and the client is one that surpasses the level of single theoretic models and it is the key for a 'successful' therapy, despite the essential conceptual separation of different therapeutic modalities. In the relationship with the client, the therapist follows the value of human dignity, he accepts and respects a person in all of his uniqueness and entity, and he does not announce or control his behaviour.

Final statements and interpretation

The analysis of the material confirms *the concept of sexually conditional and socio-culturally acceptable behaviours of psychical crises manifestations*. Men and women adjust psychical distress to a specific socio-cultural environment and to sexually acceptable behavioural patterns.

Women's mental health problems are closely linked to their social role; they are a network of past educational patterns and consolidate external expectations. Mental pain manifests itself in forms that are attributed to women and are the consequence of socialization and later life experiences connected to it. Women express personal dissatisfaction within the accorded sexual roles and a determined cultural context. The form of mental pain manifestation is the result of the 'female" socialization. Women express personal dissatisfaction with a silent, inconspicuous 'female' behaviour (Podgornik 2001, 136).

The anthropologist Darja Zaviršek (1993, 104,105) establishes that depression as a behavioural cultural pattern is a typical manifestation of mental pain, which "is attributed to the female sex, creates different sexual ideologies and leads many women with a sexually acceptable behavioural pattern to identify themselves with it and to adapt the expression of their psychical distress to it". Resorting to a disease is also frequent; addiction to pills, addiction to alcohol and addiction to food (refusing food, excessive eating, overeating and then throwing up and combinations of those), coffee, and cigarettes are socially more acceptable for women.

The concept of factors that that are conditional to the formation of psychical crises is also connected to the socio-cultural environment. The intertwinement of negative factors like class appurtenance, patriarchal sexual pattern, national appurtenance, physical violence, wrong care work, a long period of living in a threatening and stressful relationship, unemployment, and people's socio-economic problems are the basis for the manifestation of mental health problems.

From the presented socio-biographies it is obvious that the perception and performing of male and female roles is connected to the gender[47] as a socially constructed category, but not their sensibility for a social construction of both genders. In other words, they understand their actions as a biological determination of their sexual identity.

Their social roles do not deviate essentially from the ones defined on the basis of a biological function. Women realize their role of a family and home guardian and educator, while men preserve the role of a family provider and the family representative in the public

---

[47] Curran and Renzetti define "sex" as a biologically given gender, and the "gender" is a social category built on its basis. The biological gender divides humanity into men and women, while the social gender represents manhood or womanhood (Curran and Renzetti 1995, 2).

sphere. Compared to women, men benefit from a superior position. The convictions and actions of the clients reflect a traditional course of socialization, favouring social roles regarding the biological gender. Their sexual identity is the result of commonly adopted norms and values of the culture that they belong to. They act appropriately in socially acceptable roles in view of the gender. The qualities in the domain of the female social gender are tenderness, sensibility, excessive sentimentality, passivity, and willingness to subordinate, while the qualities in the domain of the male social gender are rationality, aggressiveness, emotional stability, and activity. This represents itself as an additional burdening in the manifestation of psychical crises. If the behaviour does not suit the qualities connected to the gender, they experience a bigger stigmatization – the case of a depressed man and an alcoholized woman.

The traditional patriarchal ideology still infuses the public and personal sphere of social activity. In the patriarchal perspective, the maternal role remains the woman's primary role. Her identification through this role is bounded to another person (father, husband, child), who in a patriarchal society is considered superior. A woman shares less personal and social strength than a man. The sexist treating of a woman, i.e. the discriminatory treatment based on gender, represents a collection of social values, roles, and expectations.[48] The female and male social genders, built on the basis of specific gender values and stereotypes, influence the formation of the female and male concept of one's own SELF.[49] Two important viewpoints of one's SELF are self-image and self-confidence, which have a crucial influence on the confirmation of one's identity (Burke 1980). In this way the socially desired and expected gendered roles, values, and types of behaviour are firmly anchored in a person's identity and in the whole social construction.

A patriarchal society dictates to a woman a behaviour in accordance with the concepts of the patriarchate, which does not allow or stigmatize actions that are not in accordance with the patriarchal relations. The influence of a patriarchal culture on a woman's mental health is visible in her experiencing and the expression of her feelings. A woman, with internalized beliefs that she should be calm, patient, indulgent, understanding, attentive, meticulous, serene, and not angry, expresses with difficulty her desires and needs and therefore she realizes them with difficulty. The frustration regarding the ascribed femininity takes place

---

[48] It is necessary to warn that sexism did not disappear, it just changed its manifestation forms and became subtler. Women's loss of privilege is passing from formal and explicit forms to informal and latent ones. According to Bourdieu (2001), sexism is an essential or indispensable construct that preserves historical-institutionalized differences between the genders, places them on the level of "biological disposition" and excuses the present social situation. It functions as a necessity which clarifies the existence of both genders. The concept of "symbolistic violence" explains the existing social differences between the genders.

[49] Burke (1980) defines SELF as a unit of ideas about ourselves, which are based on self-observation or rational deduction about who we are. The opinion is formed on the basis of how others behave towards us, our wishes and desires and our self-evaluation as well.

on a personal level, through the dissatisfaction with oneself, non-actualization of oneself in one's self-concept. [50]

Demographic factors, gender, age, marital status, ethnical appurtenance, and socio-economic status in interaction with personal qualities influence the formation of mental health problems and also their development and solving. Researchers (Pez et al. 2006) establish that the social network and relationships work as factors of chances or protective factors for the formation and development of mental problems.

The English scientists, Brown and Harris (1989) indicated as causes of mental problems disappointment in the family, conjugal fights, change of place or working place, an illness or death of a family member, financial problems, or loss of a certain social role – these kinds of occurrences are present in 30% of mental illnesses cases. They also showed that the type of negative experience does not determine the future illness as much as the meaning given to it by the affected person and his subjective alteration. The research also showed that women who have a strong, confident mutual relationship with their husband, relative, or friend are less susceptible to depression than women who did not receive that type of support in their relationships.

The importance of relationships for mental health is emphasized by the mental health condition research, which showed that individuals with mental health problems have less emotional control than those without. The decrease of emotional support networks was reported by individuals who, in the last month, felt strongly limited because of their emotional problems, in comparison to individuals who did not have these kinds of problems and to individuals who believe they have a worse control of their life in comparison to people who have the feeling that they are doing good. The data also shows that individuals with smaller social networks more often report about feelings of sadness, bad mood, depression, as well as suicidal thoughts (Kamin et al. 2009, 85).

From the present material, among the causes for the formation of mental crises, the use of actions of constraint and control as a universal characteristic of a specific behaviour on the level of interpersonal relations stands out. *The construct of external control* is typical for parents-children relationships and for relationships between two partners. These are relationships that represent an important figure in a person's world of qualities and to which great expectations are tied. The clients tried to attain these expectations with external control, in the context of universal, i.e. behavioural psychology, all to the realization that internal control is the only one possible, because people are internally (intrinsically)

---

[50] A person's self represents an integral role in the human motivation, perception, experience and social identity. Its basic attribute is reflexivity, i.e. the ability to look at oneself as an object; the ability of self-evaluation, self-referring, self-awareness of our own existence and the ability to plan future activity according to our desired goals (Stets and Burke, 2008: 5).

motivated beings, so no external motivational factor or stimulus is effective in the long term. Furthermore, the ethnographic material used in this monograph also proves that forced and controlling actions are inevitably destructive for a person and his relationships.

Controlling someone else from the position of a victim, in the role of a mother and wife, still exists in modern society. In my opinion it is linked to the existence of the patriarchal relationship in which a woman cannot appease her needs for power and value in her relationship with an insecure and non-autonomous man. However, it is not an excuse for the psychic abuse of children, which is frequently not even considered as abuse, but a traditional (Christian) education of attentive and responsible parents.

It is possible to find the source of controlling behaviours in a child's education and in men's feeling of superiority in their relationships with women, especially in the Christian religion, which is based on intimidation and punishments. The accepting and believing in the so-called fourth commandment: "Honour your father and your mother, so that you may live long in the land the Lord your God gives you", maintains the traditional relationships between parents and children and causes a sense of guilt and commitment to the parents, which is connected to hatred.

The psychic abuse of children changes its form; it passes from one extreme (little concern) to another (excessive concern) regarding their social acceptance and desirability. However, it always expresses an ineffective, even pathological, form of appeasing the parents' needs.

Research on the concept of attachment as the main dimension of the parents' characteristics, which represents the basis of interpersonal relationships, indicate parental concern or love, and protection or control (Hinde in Parker 1990; Schaefer 1965). Based on the questionnaire on relationships with parents (Parental Bonding Instrument), prepared by Parker, Tupling, and Brown (1979), studies showed that little concern and a high and excessive protection of the parents are linked to the majority of psychiatric illnesses (Parker 1983 in Parker 1990). Parker defines that so-called optimal parenting as a highly caring concern and a low excessive protection, which could be described in the context of attachment theory (Bowlby) as a safe form of attachment (of the child to the parents).

The couples therapeutic work, based on Bowlby's attachment theory takes into consideration the fact that negative internal models, which define oneself as unworthy of love and others as unworthy of trust, adverse and unloving, are not pathologic projections, but answers adapted to the experience in the original family (Erzar and Kompan Erzar 2011, 222). Attachment theory includes four types of anxious attachments, which include the anxiety of attached parents that makes the child a victim of an un-safe attachment. Bowlby shows that fear, or a supposed spoiling on the parents' part, especially the mother, has its "roots in the relationship she has with her mother, which was marked by the fear of an emotional closeness, anger, emotional manipulation and evasion" (ibid, 69).

The shift to the field of relational theory continues with the identification of the phenomenon named *protective childhood*, expressed through intensive care of children, their well-being, education, etc., (Švab 2001, 135); it strengthens and popularizes in the post-modern era. Giddens (2000 14) links the educational control with the concept of toxic parents, emotively insufficient parents, who prevent their children from developing into autonomous individuals, with a controlling education practice. It is possible to recognize the creative, destructive behaviours of children and adolescents as new forms of liberation from the parents' protective control – which also reflects in the form of torturing one's own body, for example as anorexia nervosa (Rener 1998, 62), understood in the context of choice theory as a form of exerting control over one's own body. An individual who is under control can actually control only his own body and that is a clear form of resistance to the form of control that he is experiencing, most frequently from his parents.

To a protective childhood, we can also link the phenomenon of late social maturity syndrome, also named the *postponing adulthood syndrome*. It is not connected only to economic causes that are influencing the mobility and financial independency of the young and to a distinct openness of the higher education system, but it uncovers the educational patterns of a certain society.

The second most distinct destructive controlling behaviour is violence. The results of the research carried out within a research project about family violence show that the victims of family violence are mostly women, children, and older family members. The occurrence of violence against women in a domestic environment has been increasing in the last decade, and violence against women and children ending in their deaths is increasing as well.

The most dangerous place for a woman is her home and the most dangerous individual is her partner. At the same time, the low level of recognising the violence against women and the high level of tolerance regarding domestic violence are very alarming.

The socially acceptable and tolerated aggressive behaviour, characteristic of a general culture, remains a fixed educational pattern. Punishment and the use of the three Cs (criticism, correction, coercion) are the most common behaviours that parents chose in their relationship with a child. Control psychology behaviours give children the feeling of being controlled, suppressed, and slowed down, and stimulate the development of rebelliousness and self-criticism (Primason 2004, 35). Even among modern education approaches, which are still based on two key tools for managing others – punishment and reward – the external control psychology behaviours are not recognized as unwanted and damaging. The controlling behaviours in school and the domestic sphere are destroying personal relationships with destructive behaviours, and are preventing individuals from successfully appeasing their psychic needs, which manifest in the so-called problematic behaviours of young people.

The analysis of the gathered ethnographic materials shows interactions in the manifestation of psychic crises, among the factors which condition the formation of psychic crises and are attached to the nation's psychology, and also the client's personal characteristics (thinking, experiencing, and understanding problems).

Despite the individuality of the actions, the defined concepts (autonomy, responsibility, destructive thinking and actions, controlling behaviour, searching in others (people, environment …) for reasons of one's own dissatisfaction, avoiding a direct involvement in a present dissatisfaction, the position of a victim, helplessness, orientating towards suffering, and others) and the strongly stressed problems with unsatisfying relationships with close persons (a bad relationship with an important person, the lack of connection with people, loneliness, social isolation, the lack of relationships, the attempt to change another person, the attempt to restrict/prevent the appeasing of needs, a small network of social relationships, the attempt to control another person, and others) can be easily transferred from the level of interpersonal relationships to a socio-cultural level.

A national identity is also linked to the *construct of creative behaviour*. For the present research, we chose only some forms of expressing dissatisfaction, which represent clearly enough the human creative system and their social acceptance. We defined behaviour as an (unsuccessful) attempt to satisfy the basic needs. With frustration (which occurs every time we cannot satisfy our needs), the system (immune, cardiovascular …) becomes destructive-creative. People who cannot find a way to regain a successful control over their own lives or, for any reason, do not want to renounce unsatisfying relationships, keep the behaviour offered by their creative system – psychopathology, psychosomatic, autoimmune diseases, neurosis, and similar[51] (Glasser 1998, 144–145, 149).

The reason why we perceive a great part of reality (life situations) differently than others is in our personal world, in the *construct of our quality world* (Glasser), which belongs to each individual, and in the *construct of individual differences*. The individual world, which everyone starts to create soon after birth and continues to do so all their life, is composed by specific images, figures, specific forms of appeasing the basic needs for which we strive our whole lives. This world includes the people we love, the things we like to experience, and the ideas or belief systems that regulate most of our behaviour. The presented therapeutic

---

[51] People who chose this form of behaviour, do not deny reality as people who have psychosis do, but they have problems facing it – phobias, anxieties, panicking, obsessions, compulsive or post-traumatic stress are the most common cases of these creative choices (Glasser, 1998: 158).

processes take into consideration the fact that, besides biological differences and different environments in which individuals live, our personal development is strongly influenced by individual behavioural choices, that people with different biological endowment and different environments choose. Individuals develop specific quality worlds which again influence the diversity of people (Lojk 1999, 19). An individual's mental health is directly linked to his personal, individual world. He reaches his well-being when a choice in the real world is close to the image from his quality world; the greater the deviation of the real image from the desired one, the greater is a person's level of frustration. He tries to reduce the frustration by choosing behaviours, which according to Glasses, are always holistic and intentional, regardless of their expedience or destructiveness (Glasser 1998, 55).

Choice theory defines *the construct of holistic behaviour* as a simultaneous activity of four components: activity, thinking, feeling, and physiology (ibid, 80). Although by choosing the holistic behaviour all four components still function, a person has direct control over his activities and his thinking, while feeling and physiology depend on the two of them (ibid, 81–82). That is why the holistic behaviour (mentally and physically), even if unusual and pathological, of a disease (except when it is caused by a proved organic pathology) in the organismic sense is always intentional (Lojk and Lojk 2011, 313). The integrity of a behaviour, when the change in one component – especially the key change of a belief – represents the change of the holistic behaviour, is thoroughly described in the therapeutic process recordings.

The pathogenetic and salutogenetic aspect explains and bases everything with the espoused theory, choice theory, on the *construct of mutual relationships*, *the construct of basic needs*, and *the motivation construct*. According to the material studied, choosing a creative destructive behaviour is explicitly linked to an individual's problems with personal relationships or unappeased needs (of love, sense of belonging, attention, value, etc.) in important relationships. The therapeutic process, whose goal is the client's regaining of control over his life, is focused on the improvement of existing or the establishment of more satisfying relationships.

The belief that we all have the same needs and that we differentiate only according to what we want to accomplish (which goal we try to reach), and on the means we use (what behaviours we choose) shows itself in the clients' presented stories, which also give us an insight into the direct connection between the construct of needs and the motivational construct. Individual images, figures and innate basic needs are the human motivator; this is why the behaviour is always intentional and pro-active, used to appease the basic needs through images from the quality world, which explain the motivation by forces originating from himself.

The reality therapists Darja Boben Bardutzky and Radovan Zupančič (2003 100) explain that the basic principle of the motivational process is based on the assumption that the responsibility and the capacity to change belong to the client, the therapist's job is to create the circumstances that would trigger the client's own motivation and agreeing to the changes. The motivational process wants to stimulate the intrinsic motivation for changes, which lead a person to the path of accepting, starting, and persisting in exertions essential for changing a behaviour. The authors indicate a few basic principles of the authors Miller and Rollnick, which enable the actualization of the intrinsic motivation. They include the expressing of empathy (including the respect of the client's freedom of choice and self-guiding, listening, subtle persuasion while bearing in mind that the choice belongs to the client, reflective listening, and judging), facing disharmony (the client's perception of disharmony between where he is and where he wants to be), avoiding arguing (while treating the disharmony, both the therapist and the client could pass over to defence strategies — the therapist uses other strategies in order to help the client see the ineffectiveness of his behaviour, but he does not force him to admit a diagnostic label, and does not try to prove and convince him with force or other coercive behaviours that would make the client resist and increase his defence from chance), controlling reluctance (he talks openly, directly about his problem, but not bluntly, frontally), and stimulating self-effectiveness (the client must be sure that he is capable of changing his behaviour and removing his problems) (ibid, 100–101). [52]

With the construct of basic needs, we do not connect only from the viewpoint of the interactivity of the components of holistic behaviour, but also destructive *basic convictions*. Aaron Beck (2005) talks about two of the most basic beliefs – the basic belief that we are not loved (the need for love and belonging), and the basic belief that we are not competent (the need for power and validity). According to the cognitive behavioural model, our basic convictions[53], during specific life events, trigger automatic thoughts, which can also have a dysfunctional effect – they can cause an unpleasant feeling, despite the fact that they can be completely distorted and / or wrong. In that case, an individual's perception differs from a desired image of oneself or of a situation, and so he inevitably experiences a frustration. This leads to a reorganized behaviour (Glasser), to the loss of control over one's own life, and to the system's creativity – the formation of mental health problems.

---

[52] The presented aspects are included in the reality therapy. We put into parentheses some parallel thoughts.

[53] Aaron Beck (1995) formed, with his co-workers, a scheme of characteristic "thought mistakes" as perceiving events in only two extreme categories (black/white) and not in a continuum; catastrophizing: a negative prediction of the future without taking into consideration the real circumstances; disqualification and exclusion of positivity; emotional judgment; labelling – we ascribe ourselves or others a simplified quality; glorifying/ minimalizing oneself, others, situations; mental filter – we do not see the whole picture; personalization – an egocentric and subjective interpretation, etc.

The explanation that people are responsive beings is the basis of *the external control psychology*, as Glasser names a group of destructive behaviours, based on the false belief that it is possible to control another person's behaviour. With the mass use of traditional psychology, Glasser connects numerous unhappy relationships and of course persons who cannot satisfy their basic needs in unsatisfying relationships. In opposition to the external control theory, *the internal control theory* or the theory of personal freedom (Glasser) asserts that a man consciously chooses his most complex behaviour connected to a personal system of values (images in the quality world). Consequently, he can also choose connective behaviours that enable him to establish and maintain satisfying relationships within which he will be able to appease more successfully his psychical needs.

From the viewpoint of the internal control theory, the *illness theory* also explains an illness in the light of the reality therapy, that a client's symptomatic behaviour is not caused by pathologic organic changes, but it is about the client's unhappiness which manifests itself through the chosen symptomatology. He interprets unhappiness as loneliness, a lack of relationships or unsatisfying relationships. The client's dissatisfaction originates from his comprehension that other people or external circumstances cause him suffering, which is why he perceives himself as a victim, without any power or influence to make better choices. The client tries to establish control over his life, by changing other persons' behaviour even when they are not willing to do so. The client tries to change a person's behaviour and adapt it to his desires and needs through behaviours like criticizing, accusing, complaining, whining, bribing, extorting, threatening, punishing, etc., the sort of behaviours that cannot make a person change his behaviour and could have a destructive effect on the relationship.

When the client cannot find the right choice with the thinking or active component of behaviour with which he would be able to satisfy his basic needs more effectively, his creative system offers solutions with different emotional and physiological behaviours (symptoms). Choice theory teaches us that symptomatic behaviours are merely additional attempts of the organism to lower the frustration. The therapeutic process in reality therapy implies a self-estimation of the disharmony between the client's words and his actions, a self-estimation of the connection between his actions and their consequences, (self-) estimation, (self-) examining of the client with the therapist's support, how his convictions and his actions prove to be effective in practice within relationships in which he lives, judgment and self-judgment of not knowing new and different ways of behaviour that choice theory offers. The help process is focused on learning how to substitute the external control psychology by using the more effective choice theory. In reality therapy the responsibility is clearly delineated and it is not identified by the actions of others, but by what we are prepared to do by ourselves within our roles, to approach and to offer as much choice as possible. The choice is made by the individual autonomously and so he is responsible for it. In this context, he is also responsible for taking over the control over his life once again.[54]

Regarding the 'curative' theory, reality therapy with a constructive and systematic theoretical background certainly does not have a universal method of guiding the therapeutic process, but it originates from a defined structure that is based on an authentic relationship between the therapist and the client. The therapist, working with the client, tracks axioms of choice therapy: that we are not externally motivated, but internally, that all the important behaviours are chosen, that we are responsible for our behaviour, and that there are still plenty of possible solutions. During the discussion, the therapist shifts the client's attention from the past to the present, from others to himself (we cannot control other persons' behaviour, but we can control ours), from circumstances to his own behaviour, from emotions and physiology to actions and thinking, to behavioural components, which we control directly – in the way of changing what he wants (the changing of images into the quality world) and/or changing what he does (actual holistic behaviour).

It is possible to summarize two more concepts from the analysis of the material, connected to the help model that the clients received. *The concept of the medical help model* is based on the discovering and on the interpretation of symptoms and it defines their treatment. The main instrument is a pharmacological treatment, where a psychological approach does not have any special meaning. The medical model defends the conviction that mental disturbances are a product of biochemical changes that can be treated with a pharmacological therapy. By not taking into consideration the person's individual and socio-cultural background of his psychic crisis, the medical model does not recognize the need for a holistic treatment which would include also a psychosocial approach to treatment. The advocates for the social model define the medical one as ineffective, for which the "similarity" concept is typically used, where various distinctions apply without taking into consideration the person and his socio-biography. Psychiatric hospitalization can lead to numerous iatrogenic injuries [55], cited by Tanja Lamovec, psychologist and supporter of the use of psychiatric services: dependence on drugs, lifelong stigmatization, lowered self-respect and self-confidence, strengthening a fake self, repression of genuine feeling and expressing, different relationships with family and friends, and different relationships in a workplace and loss of life goals (Lamovec 1995, 34).

The concept of the psychosocial help model, which does not use medical diagnoses, but contextual descriptions of problems and disturbances, originated as a critique of the medical model. We should accentuate the systematic-ecological (holistic) concept that developed in the

---

[54] In the choice theory terminology, an effective control means that with our behaviour we are appeasing the images of our quality world in a satisfying way.

[55] These are injuries caused by a treatment or an environment linked to it.

seventies and is based on systematic theory – on the understanding of effective connections and interactions among people and their relation towards the environment in which they live. While solving the problem, the client (user) is an active participant, capable of solving his own distress and taking control over his life with professional help.[56] In the eighties, the socio-constructivist model, connected to humanism and existentialism, starts to develop with social constructivism. With this model the basic disciplines used are sociology, cognitive psychology, linguistics, anthropology, etc., and the client (user) is an expert in recognizing his own life situation. *Reality therapy*, substantiated by choice theory that I established as the contextual and interpretative theory of the present monograph, belongs among psychotherapeutic approaches with a constructivist and systematic background.

We conclude the attempt to form theoretic concepts with *the therapist–client relationship*, which represents the expedient and purpose in reality therapy. The client (and the therapist) senses in the most genuine relationships how the subject-object relationship changes into the subject-subject relationship. In the therapist-client relationship we are not concerned with the question of 'transfer' and 'contra transfer' as a process that in psychoanalysis enables the client to comprehend, and as a process that a psychoanalyst should be conscious of in order to avoid eventual problems in the relationship between him and the client. Reality therapy believes that a responsible personal connection between the therapist and the client is the best, the fastest, and frequently also the only way for the client to learn how to develop his relationships with the people he needs (Lojk 1999, 9).

---

[56] From this point of view, there is a big gap between the systematic-ecologic theory and the radical theory, which finds the causes for the manifestation of psychosocial problems in the social system, and the opportunities for eliminating them in the modification of social structures, which exonerate the person from his partial responsibility for the phenomenon and from solving crises.

FINAL NOTE

The basic paradigmatic frame of the monograph *Mental Health in Modern Society* is health anthropology, which is based on the assumption that health and illness are social constructs, while their manifestations are part of the cultural patterns of a defined society. Assuming that expressing personal distress represents a response to a person's riskiness, uncertainty, and disconnection in modern society, we do not strip the person, as a subject, of his co-responsibility for the formation of psychic crises, but we concentrate the research on his perception and behaviour, linked to beliefs (which are the product of a cultural context and social behaviour), on the subject's opportunity to actualize himself, regardless of the social and cultural determination of psychic crises. Thinking about health separately from illness demands a deviation from universal psychology, which is based on classical conditionality (stimulus-reaction) and instrumental conditionality (rewarding, punishing), originating from external (extrinsic) motivation.

The paradigmatic move was performed in dealing with problems with mental health based on a dialogue between anthropology, sociology, and psychotherapy, which enables us to see a person and to consider him as a holistic being, with all his physical, psychical, social, and mental extensions and his position in a socio-cultural environment.

The professional and social perception of the mental health entity in connection with mental illness preserves and confirms the medical model, based on discovering and interpreting symptoms, and defining their treatment. Traditional psychiatry often denies the connection between everyday life events and mental health problems. But health anthropology defines medical treatment as a social practice, which takes into consideration a person's social context, gender differences, and the connection between personal and social. Through basic concepts and discourses like gender and culture, health anthropology emphasizes the characteristics of social systems, values, and manifestations of social distress. Besides the perception of health and illness, it offers a perspective on a person in a highly industrialized society and the culture as a whole.

We cannot understand a person's mental health problems without taking into consideration the social and cultural frames of his experiencing and expressing.

From this point of view, we try to define mental health as a part of good interpersonal relationships, social networks, quality of life, satisfactory self-image, and satisfying strategies for mastering the distresses in contrast with the negative concepts of mental health. Along with that, we take into consideration the individual's personal history and biography, included in the research work, the socio-demographic and socioeconomic factors of the influence on mental health, outside of the medical treatment of mental health as the absence of mental illness.

The conviction of the indivisibility of mental and physical dictates a holistic and proactive understanding of a person's activity, which is why an approach oriented towards an individual is necessary. With the completed research work, I want to contribute to recognizing the need for a holistic approach in treating psychical crises, by placing a person's inter-subjective social world into a larger socio-cultural context.

We recognize the present research as research into interpersonal relations, into a modern society person's holistic behaviour, and his response to the pain connected to the risks that it brings to modern society. The material we studied is rich and it enables the recognizing of numerous social threads – socialization patterns, patriarchy, matriarchy, differences between genders, and other factors that determined the origin of psychical distresses, a person's creative system, reorganized behaviours as a response to personal crises, and an individual's other attempts to regain control over his life.

Despite studying the problematic from the viewpoint of the axioms of the chosen theory, we satisfied the humanistic ideas that every individual and every situation are unique and they need to be treated and understood in their own uniqueness. A personal psychotherapeutic approach did not just enable us to focus on a general understanding, but we had also to remain in a position of special understanding, and acknowledge an individual's uniqueness. The analyzing, connecting, and interpreting of the special enabled the presentation of a broader (public) mental health of the modern population, the manifestation forms, and (ineffective and painful) ways of solving problems.

We analyzed a person's behaviour and thinking in relation to the environment and the persons that the client co-creates his life with. We researched two fields: the happenings in a person and in a (domestic) environment. Separately – individually became the social cultural perspective.

The research I carried out problematizes the conventional consideration of behaviouristic psychology as a universal science. It confirmed the discovery that universal psychology preserves all of its strength in all important human relationships and social systems. It is shown that the most prominent relationships regarding the controlling of someone else's behaviour are in fact the relationships with a partner, relationships within a family, and those in school and in a workplace, and that even the most appeased existential needs cannot replace the neglected psychic needs of a person, a social being, for whom the concept of establishing and maintaining a good relationship with others is necessary (from the perspective of needs and mere survival).

The analysis of the case study enabled the testing of the hypothesis and the reliability of the confirmation. The cases represent the theoretical process of an illness and its treatment. The uncovering of subtle aspects and the characteristics of people with mental health problems form a "diagnosis" explaining that "all long-term psychological problems are in fact linked to relationships problems" (Glasser, 1998: 326).

Fromm believes that "a person is alone and at the same time connected. He is alone because he is a unique being, equal to nobody, who is aware of oneself as a separate being. [...] But he cannot bear the fact of being alone, of not being connected to people. His happiness depends on the reciprocity he feels towards other people [...] (Fromm 2002, 42). Fromm's assertion that "total loneliness is insufferable and incompatible with mental health", (ibid, 53) is similar to Glasser's assertion that a common problem of all people with a mental illness diagnosis is their unhappiness, especially their involvement in unhappy relationships (Glasser 2006, 15).

According to our anthropological stance, we, as people, need each other in order to meet our needs and desires. The entire human life is placed in a concrete biophysical, psychic, and social endowment. Roger's definition of a relationship enables the individual to "fully function" (Evans 1975). This kind of relationship is qualitative; the individual is understood as a person with the possibility of personal growth – self-actualization, which is an authentic characteristics of the human organism (ibid).

The result of the assumption that perception and consciousness are constructions and not registrations of the "external" world means that the human perception changes with the changing of the nature of the constructional process (Ornstein 1973). A person's freedom is present in the making of his own conscious choices among various possibilities within the concrete situations, endowments and restrictions. The possibility of choosing and deciding for himself enables a renewed evaluation of an individual's personal freedom – "we have more personal freedom if we are ready to replace external control psychology with the choice theory", believes Glasser (2007a 293).

That is why I understand the existing "risk society" merely as a framework within which "a person is the one who creates reality and also himself by doing so" (Berger and Luckmann

1988, 169). The belief of humanistic-existential philosophy is that human behaviour is not controlled by external events, but it is motivated exclusively by forces that originate from himself (Glasser 1998). Blaming an "external factor" for a person's unhappiness comes from the general belief that his behaviour is a reaction to external stimuli and that his "feeling is caused by other people and events" (ibid, 3), while he has no possibility to decide otherwise.

The liberation of fundamental social forms of industrial society – class, family, and gender roles (Beck 2001, 105–106) – increases the choices and enables the individual's self-actualization. Undoubtedly, an important consequence of individualization is the post-modern individual's constant search for his identity (Cova 1999, 72), but it is in the constant search for the meaning of his life that it is necessary to search for the individual's freedom and his possibility to actualize himself more than he could "within a fixed social and cultural form of community and family that created the subjects' identities from the outside, and imposed to the individual a stable status position in a determined space and time. These persons were not individuals in the modern sense of the word; their personality was based on the collective meaning of identity, their will was directed according to traditional and untouchable moral rules, their consciousness was not the consciousness of unique individuals, but of persons with defined destinies. With the modern period, the relocation from countryside to the city, the passage from stability and fixation to change and fluidity, from feudalism and farming to capitalism, trade production and business with the labour force, a person gained a new form: he became a unique, conscious, responsible, automatized, discrete, bounded, coherent, choosing, active individual, with a personal consciousness and a personal conscience. This person is at the same time a subject of freedom and responsibility." (Rose 1997, 138)

In the democratization of individualization, it is about searching for a person's opportunity to successfully form and realize his life story by being conscious of free choice, liberated from the restraints that determined his lifestyle in the past. A person is the one that creates the nucleus of every human action with his own experiencing, and an individual is the active subject that we cannot put in the place of an object, if we want them to preserve his human values.

At the end of the humanistic-sociological debate about identity therapy, Berger and Luckmann ask themselves: "Why would one type of psychology replace another during the course of history?", and they offer a general answer that "such change takes place when, for any reason, the identity becomes problematic. This can sprout from the dialectics of psychological reality and social structure. [...] In this case, new psychological theories can appear, because the old empirical phenomena cannot be properly explained anymore." (Berger and Luckmann 1988, 165).

The theses of choice theory are linked to today's predominant liberal ideology of an individual who can realize himself and control his life. From the prospective of an individual's psychology, we can deduce that the person is autonomically and self-sufficiently treated, but choice theory emphasizes the meaning of a fellow human being for a person's actualization and the meaning of their satisfying relationship. Just as much, it represents the possibility for a renewed evaluation of an individual's personal freedom and creation of a quality society.

LITERATURE AND SOURCES

Adams, Lee, Amos, Mary in Munro, James F (2002) *Promoting Health. Politics and Practice.* London, Thousand Oaks, New Delhi: Sage Publications.

Adler, A. (1999) *Smisel življenja.* Ljubljana: Fors, Založba Sophia.

Andrews, Frank M. in Stephen B. Withey (1976/1978) *Social Indicators of Well-Being:*

American Perceptions of Life Quality. New York: Plenum Press.

Antonovsky, Aaron (1991) The Structural Sources of Salutogenic Strengths. V: Cooper, Cary L. in Payne, Roy (ur.) *Personality and Stress: Individual Differences in the Stress Process.* Chichester: John Wiley & Sons, 67–102

Asch, E. Solomon (1952) *Social Psychology.* New York: Prentice Hall.

Babič, Karolina (2005) *Utopija nove humanistične družbe.* Dialogi, 9, 81.

Bahovec, Igor (2005) *Skupnosti : teorije, oblike, pomeni.* Ljubljana: Sophia.

Bauman, Zygmunt (2002) *Tekoča moderna.* Ljubljana: *Cf.*

Bauman, Zygmunt (2007) *Consuming Life.* Oxford: Polity Press.

Beck, Aaron (2005) *Cognitive Therapy - Basics and Beyond.* New York: The Guilford Press.

Beck, Ulrich (1994) *Reflexive Modernization: Politics, Tradition and Aesthetics in the Modern Social Order.* Cambridge: Polity Press.

Beck, Ulrich (1998) The Politics of Risk Society. Cambridge: Polity Press.

Beck, Ulrich (2001) *Družba tveganja: na poti v neko drugo moderno.* Ljubljana: Krtina.

Beck, Ulrich (2003) *Kaj je globalizacija?: Zmote globalizma – odgovori na*

Globalizacijo. Ljubljana: Krtina.

Beck, Ulrich in Elisabeth Beck-Gernsheim (2006) *Popolnoma normalni kaos ljubezni.* Ljubljana: Fakulteta za družbene vede.

Berger, Peter L. in Luckmann, Thomas (1988) *Družbena konstrukcija realnosti : razprava iz sociologije znanja.* Ljubljana: Cankarjeva založba.

Berger, Peter L. in Luckmann, Thomas (1999) *Modernost, pluralizem in kriza smisla : orientacija modernega človeka*. Ljubljana: Nova revija.

Bernardes, Jon (1997) *Family Studies: An Introduction.* London: Routledge.

Boben Bardutzky, Darja in Zupančič, Radovan (2003) *Realitetna terapija, odvisnosti in čudeži*. Zbornik Študijskih dnevov SKZP.

Bourdieu, Pierre (2001) *Masculine Domination.* California: Stanford University Press.

Bradburn, Norman M. in David Caplovitz (1965) *Reports on happiness: a pilot study of*

behavior related to mental health. Chicago: Aldine

Brown, George W. in Harris, Tirril (1989) S*ocial Origins of Depression. A Study of Psychiatric Disorder in Women.* London: Routledge.

Buss, A.H., & Briggs, S.R. (1984) Drama and Self in Social Interaction. *Journal of Personality and Social Psychology*, 47(6), 1310–1324.

Burke, Peter J. (1980) The Self: Measurement Implications from a Interactionist Perspective. *Social Psychology Quarterly*, 43, 18–29.

Burr, Vivien (1995) *An Introduction to Social Constructionism.* London, New York: Routledge.

Carnes P. J. (1991) *Don't Call it Love: Recovery from Sexual Addiction.* New York: Bantam Books.

Cova, Bernard (1999) From Marketing to Societing: When the Link is More Important than the Thing. V: Brownlie Douglas, Saren Mike, Wensley Robin, Whittington Richard (ur.) *Rethinking Marketing: Towards Critical Marketing Accountings.* London, Thousand Oaks, New Delhi: SAGE Publications, 64–84.

Čačinovič Vogrinčič, Gabi (2000) Vzpostavljanje in ohranjanje svetovalnega odnosa: postmoderno v terapiji in svetovanju. *Psihološka obzorja*, 9, 2, 81–86.

Doise, W. (1986) *Levels of Explanation in Social Psychology*. Cambridge, London: Cambridge Univ. Press.

Driscoll, Mary (2007) Obeti družboslovnega raziskovanja. V: Charles. C. Ragin. *Družboslovno raziskovanje. Enotnost in raznolikost metode.* Ljubljana: FDV.

Dunning, Eric (1999) Sport Matters: Sociological Studies of Sport, Violence and Civilization. London and New York: Routledge, Taylor and Francis Group.

Mental health in Europe (2018) European Commission.

Elias, Norbert (2000) *O procesu civiliziranja* (prvi zvezek). Ljubljana: Založba *cf.

Elias, Norbert (2001) *O procesu civiliziranja* (drugi zvezek). Ljubljana: Založba *cf.

Erzar, Tomaž in Kompan Erzar, Katarina (2011) *Teorija navezanosti.* Celje: Celjska Mohorjeva družba, Društvo Mohorjeva družba.

Evans, R. I. (1975) *Carl Rogers: the Man and His Ideas.* New York: Dutton.

Evans, R. I. (1988) *Graditelji psihologije.* Beograd: Nolit.

Felson, B. Richard (1993) The Effects of Self-Appraisals of Ability on Academic Performance. *Journal of Personality Social Psychology*, 47, 944–952.

Fikfak, Jurij, Adam, Frane, Garz, Detlef (ur.) (2004) *Qualitative research.* Ljubljana: Založba ZRC.

Flaker, Vito (1997) Preoblikovanje jezika duševnega zdravja. *Altra*, 2 (1): 3–5

Foucault, Michel (1975) *The Birth of Clinic: an Archaeology of Medical Perception.* New

York: Vintage Books.

Foucault, Michel (1984) *Nadzorovanje in kaznovanje.* Ljubljana: Delavska enotnost.

Friebe, Margarete (1993) *Moč moje podzavesti.* Ljubljana: Alpha center.

Freeman, Howard E. in Giovannoni, Jeanne M. (1969) Social Psychology of Mental Health. V: Aronson, Elliot in Gardner, Lindzey (ur.) *The Handbook of Social Psychology*, 5, 660–719.

Friedman, S. (1994) *Humanistic psychology overview*. Alameda: Association for Humanistic Psychology.

Fromm, Erich (2002) Človek za sebe. *Psihološka raziskava etike*. Ljubljana: Amalietti & Amalietti.

Fromm, Erich (2004) *Imeti ali biti*. Ljubljana: Vale –Novak.

Gergen, K. J. (1991) *The Saturated Self*. New York: Basic Books.

Giddens, Anthony (1991) *Modernity and Self-Identity: Self and Society in the Late Modern Age*. California: Stanford University Press.

Giddens, Anthony (1992) *The Consequences of Modernity*, Cambridge: Polity Press.

Giddens, Anthony (2000). *Preobrazba intimnosti*. Ljubljana: *Cf.

Glaser, B. G. in Strauss, A. L. (1967) *The Discovery of Grounded Theory*. Chicago: Aldine Publishing Company.

Glasser, William (1994) *Kontrolna teorija ali kako vzpostaviti učinkovito kontrolo nad svojim življenjem*. Ljubljana: Taxus.

Glasser, William (1998) *Teorija izbire*. Radovljica: TOP regionalni izobraževalni center.

Glasser, William (1998a) *How the Brain Works. Why and how we behave*. Chatsworth: The William Glasser Institute.

Glasser, William (2000) *Counseling with Choice Theory: The New Reality Therapy*. Los Angeles: Quill.

Glasser, William (2003) Counseling with Choice Theory. New York: HarperCollins Publishers.

Glasser, William (2006) *Duševno zdravje – problem javnega zdravja: nova vloga svetovalcev in psihoterapevtov*. Ljubljana: Društvo za realitetno terapijo.

Glasser, William (2007) *Kako vzpostaviti učinkovit nadzor nad svojim življenjem : teorija nadzora.* Ljubljana: samozaložba A. Urbančič.

Glasser, William (2007a) *Nova psihologija osebne svobode : teorija izbire.* Ljubljana: Louisa.

Hammersley, Martin (1992) *What's Wrong With Ethnography? Methodological Explorations.* London, New York: Routledge.

Goffman, Erving (1959) *The Presentation of Self in Everyday Life.* London: Penguin Group.

Goffman, Erving (1981) *Stigma: Notes on the Management of Spoiled Identity.* Harmondsworth: Penguin Books.

Gurin, *P.,* in Markus, *H. (1988)* Group identity: The psychological mechanisms of durable salience. *Revue Internationale de Psychologie Sociale,* 1, 257–274.

Hribar, Tine (1983) *Drama hrepenenja: (od Cankarjeve do Šeligove Lepe Vide).* Ljubljana: Mladinska knjiga.

Inkeles, Alex (1998*) One World Emerging? Convergence and Divergence in Industrial Societies.* Boulder: Westview Press

Kamin, Tanja, Jeriček, Klanšček Helena, Zorko, Maja, Bajt, Maja, Roškar, Saška, Dernovšek, Mojca Zvezdana (2009) *Duševno zdravje prebivalcev Slovenije.* Ljubljana: Inštitut za varovanje zdravja.

Kaplan, Robert M., Sallis, James F. in Patterson, Thomas L. (1993) *Health and Human Behavior.* New York: McGraw-Hill.

Kavčič, Matic (2011) *Družbena in individualna tveganja starejših – vloga omrežij socialne opore.* Doktorska disertacija. Ljubljana: Univerza v Ljubljani, Fakulteta za družbene vede.

Kobal Grum, Darja (2003) *Bivanja samopodobe.* Ljubljana: I2.

Kobolt, Alenka in Rapuš Pavel, Jana (2009) *Razumevanje in ocenjevanje čustvenih in vedenjskih težav v odraščanju.* Ljubljana: Pedagoška fakulteta.

Kores Plesničar, Blanka (2004) *Značilnosti depresije po starosti in spolu.*

Kovačič, Matjaž (2008) Vedenje o vedênju V: *Organizacija znanja,* 13, 3.

Lamovec, Tanja in Flaker, Vito (1993*) Kaj je duševna bolezen. V: Socialno delo, 3/4, 87–92.*

Lamovec, Tanja (1995) *Ko rešitev postane problem in zdravilo postane strup.* Ljubljana: Lumi.

Lamovec, Tanja (1999) *Kako misliti drugačnost.* Ljubljana: Visoka šola za socialno delo.

Lavrič, Miran in Klanjšek, Rok (2011) Stanovanjske in bivalne razmere mladih. V: Lavrič, Miran et. al.: *Mladina 2010. Družbeni profil mladih v Sloveniji.* Ljubljana: Ministrstvo za šolstvo in šport, Urad RS za mladino; Maribor: Aristej, 347–373.

Lojk, Bosiljka in Lojk, Leon (2011) Realitetna terapija. V: Žvelc, Maša, Možina, Miran in Bohak, Janko *Psihoterapija.* Ljubljana: Inštitut za integrativno psihoterapijo in svetovanje, 311-333.

Lojk, Leon (1997) Kratek prikaz realitetne terapije. V: *Svet kakovosti*, 3, 4–9.

Lojk, Leon (1999) Znanstvena utemeljenost realitetne terapije. V: *Svet kakovosti*, 5 (1), 7–47.

Lojk, Leon (2000) Znanstvena utemeljenost realitetne terapije. V: *Svet kakovosti*, 6 (1), 34–46

Leon Lojk (2001) Realitetna terapija. *Prvi študijski dnevi Slovenske krovne zveze za psihoterapijo.*

Lojk, Leon in Lojk Bosiljka (2001) Z realitetno terapijo do boljših odnosov. *Prvi študijski dnevi Slovenske krovne zveze za psihoterapijo.*

Lojk, Leon (2002) Modalitete: Realitetna terapija. *Dnevi Slovenske krovne zveze za psihoterapijo.*

Lojk, Leon (2007) Spremna beseda. V: *Kako vzpostaviti učinkovit nadzor nad svojim življenjem : teorija nadzora.* Ljubljana: samozaložba A. Urbančič.

Lojk Leon in Lojk Bosiljka (2011) Inštitut za realitetno terapijo. *Izobraževanje iz realitetne terapije.*

Lojk, Leon (2012) Osebnost v realitetni terapiji. *Kairos*, 6, 1/2, 105–114

Luhmann, Niklas (1990) Zamenjava paradigme v sistemski teoriji. *Nova revija*, 9, 761–824.

Luhmann, Niklas (1997) Pojem rizika. Časopis za kritiko znanosti, XXV, 183.

Mauss, Marcel in Levi Strauss, Claude (1996) *Esej o daru in drugi spisi*. Ljubljana: ŠKUC, Znanstveni inštitut filozofske fakultete, Studia Humanitatis.

Mead, George Herbert (1934) *Mind, Self and Society*. Chicago: University of Chicago Press.

Mead, George Herbert (1997) *Um, sebstvo, družba*. Ljubljana: Krtina.

Merkle, Rolf (1996) *Tako postanemo samozavestnejši*. Celje: Mavrica,

Mesec, Blaž (1998) *Uvod v kvalitativno raziskovanje v socialnem delu*. Ljubljana: Visoka šola za socialno delo.

Miller, Alice (2005) *Upor telesa. Telo terja resnico*. Ljubljana: Tangram.

Muršič, Mitja (2010) *Znanje o čustvih za manj nasilja v šoli*. Ljubljana: Inštitut za kriminologijo pri Pravni fakulteti v Ljubljani.

Musek, Janek (1988) *Teorije osebnosti*. Ljubljana: Filozofska fakulteta.

Musek, Janek (1992) Struktura jaza in samopodobe. *Anthropos*, 3/4, 59–79.

Musek, Janek (1999) *Psihološki modeli in teorije osebnosti*. Ljubljana: Filozofska fakulteta.

Musek, Janek (2003) *Nova psihološka teorija vrednot*. Ljubljana: Inštitut za psihologijo osebnosti, Educy.

Musek, Janek (2003) Identiteta psihologije, psihološke paradigme in konstruktivizem: perspektiva socialne paradigme v psihologiji. *Psihološka obzorja*, 12 (3), 79–92.

Novak, Bogomir (2007) Antropološka kritika psihoterapije in psihiatrije.

Ornstein, R. E. (1973) *The Nature of Human Consciousness*. San Francisco: W. H Freeman and Co.

Oyserman, D. in Markus, H. R. *(1993)* The *sociocultural self.* V: Suls, J. (ur.) *Psychological perspectives* on the *self, 4*, 187–220.

Parker, G., Tupling, H. in Brown, L. B. (1979) A parental bonding instrument. *British Journal of Medical Psychology,* 52 (1), 1–10.

Parker, G. (1990) The Parental Bonding Instrument. A decade of research. *Social Psychiatry and Psychiatric Epidemiology*, 25, 281–282.

Pescitelli, Dagmar (1996) *An Analysis of Carl Rogers' Theory of Personality.*

Pez, O., Bit Foi, A., Carta M., Jordanova, V., Mateos, R., Prince, M., Tudorache, B., Gilbert, F., Kovess Safety (2006) Survey instruments and Methods. V: Lavikainen, J., Fryers, T., Lehtinen, V. (ur.) Improving Mental Health Information in Europe, 49–66.

Podgornik, Nevenka (2001) *Družbeno-kulturno ozadje manifestiranja psihičnih kriz.* Magistrska naloga. Ljubljana: ISH.

Podgornik, Nevenka (2012) Kriva je Eva. *Androcentrična konstrukcija stvarnosti in manifestiranje psihičnih kriz žensk.* Ljubljana: Vega

Powers, William T. (2005) *Behavior: The Control of Perception.* New Canaan: Benchmark Publications.

Primason, Richard (2004) *Choice Parenting. A more connecting, less controlling way to manage any child behavior problem.* New York: iUniverse, Inc.

Renzetti, M. Claire, Curran, J. Daniel (ur.) (1995) *Women, Men and Society.* Boston: Allyn and Bacon.

Rogers, Carl (1951) Client-centered Therapy: Its current practice, implications and theory. Boston: Houghton Mifflin.

Rogers, Carl (1995) *On Becoming a Person.* New York: Houghton Mifflin Company.

Rose, Nikolas (1997) Avtoriteta in genealogija subjektivnosti. Časopis za kritiko znanosti, 183, 131–159.

Rovatti, Pier Aldo (2004) *Norost v nekaj besedah.* Trst: ZTT EST.

Sande, Matej (2004) *Uporaba drog v družbi tveganj: Vpliv varovalnih dejavnikov in dejavnikov tveganja.* Ljubljana: Pedagoška fakulteta.

Sapir, Edward (1994) *The Psychology of Culture.* Berlin, New York; Mouton de Gruyer.

Schaefer, S. Earl (1965) A configurational analysis of children's reports of parent behavior. *Journal of Consulting Psychology*, 29 (6), 552–557.

Schulz von Thun, Friedemann (2001) *Kako medusobno razgovaramo*. Zagreb: Erudita.

Sedmak, Mateja, Kralj, Ana, Medarič, Zorana, Simčič, Blaž (2006) *Nasilje v družinah v Sloveniji*. Koper: Univerza na Primorskem, Znanstveno-raziskovalno središče Koper.

Shaw, Charla L. M. (1997) Personal narrative: revealing self and reflecting other. *Human communication research*, 2, 302–319.

Skalar, Marija (1990) *Pojmovanje samega sebe in samovrednotenje*. Ljubljana: Pedagoška fakulteta.

Skinner, B. F. (1953) *Science and Human Behavior*. New York: Macmillan.

Snygg, Donald in Combs, Arthur W. *(1949) Individual Behavior*: A *New Frame* of *Reference* for *Psychology*. *New* York: *Harper*.

Stein, R. Maurice, Vidich, J. Arthur in Manning-White, David (1962) *Identity and Anxiety: Survival of the Person in Mass Society*. Glencoe: The Free Press.

Stets, Jan E. in Burke Peter J. (2008) *A Sociological Approach to Self and Identity. Handbook of Self and Identity*. Washington State University.

Strauss, L. Anselm in Corbin, Juliet (1990) *Basics of Qualitative Research: Grounded Theory Procedures and Techniques*. Newbury Park: Sage.

Stražar, M. (1975*)* Nedirektivna teorija Carla R. Rogersa. V: Lamovec, T., Musek, J., Pečjak, V. (ur.) *Teorije osebnosti*. Ljubljana: Cankarjeva založba.

Sullivan, H. Stack (1953) *The Interpersonal Theory of Psychiatry*. New York: Norton.

Svetovni dan boja proti samomoru (2008) Statistični urad RS.

Szasz, Thomas S. (1960) The myth of mental illness. *American Psychologist*, 15, 113–118.

Szazs, Thomas S. (1982) *Proizvodnja ludila*. Zagreb: Grafički zavod Hrvatske, OOUR Izdavačka djelatnost.

Šugman Bohinc, Lea (2005) *Kibernetika psihoterapije – razvijanje postmoderne dialoške prakse*. Maribor: Slovenska krovna zveza za psihoterapijo.

Švab, Alenka (2001) *Družina: od modernosti k postmodernosti.* Ljubljana: Znanstveno in publicistično središče.

Tajfel, Henri in John Turner (1985) The social identity theory of intergroup behavior. V: Worcehl, S. in Austin, W. G. (ur.) *Psychology of Intergroup Relations,* 7024.

Tudor, Keith (1996) *Mental Health Promotion: Paradigms and Practice.* London, New York: Routledge.

Ule, Mirjana (1994) *Temelji socialne psihologije.* Ljubljana: Znanstveno in publicistično središče.

Ule, Mirjana (2000) *Sodobne identitete. V vrtincu diskurzov.* Ljubljana: ZPS.

Ule, Mirjana (2003) *Spregledana razmerja: o družbenih vidikih sodobne medicine.* Maribor:

Aristej.

Ule, Mirjana in Kuhar, Metka (2003) *Mladi, družina, starševstvo. Spremembe življenjskih potekov v pozni moderni.* Ljubljana: Fakulteta za družbene vede, Center za socialno psihologijo.

Ule, Mirjana (2005) *Socialna psihologija.* Ljubljana: Fakulteta za družbene vede.

Weeks, Jeffrey (1995) *Invented moralities: Sexual values in an age of uncertainty.* Cambridge: Polity Press, Blackwell Publishers Ltd.

Willke, Helmut (1993) *Sistemska teorija razvitih družb.* Ljubljana: Fakulteta za družbene vede.

White, D. (1988) Madness and Psychiatry. *Asylum,* 3 (2).

World Health Organization (2010) Mental health: strengthening our response.

Wubbolding, Robert (2000) *Reality Therapy for the 21st Century.* Philadelphia, PA: Brunner-Routledge.

Zalta, Anja, Kralja, Ana, Zurc, Joca, Lenarčič, Blaž, Medarič, Zorana, Simčič, Blaž (2008) *Mladi in alkohol v Sloveniji.* Koper: Univerza na Primorskem, Znanstveno - raziskovalno središče Koper.

Zaviršek, Darja (1993) Ženske in duševno zdravje v feministični antropologiji. *Socialno delo, Duševno zdravje v skupnosti*, 32, (1-2), 91–107.

Zaviršek, Darja (1994) *Zdravje kot sistemski del societalnosti.* Doktorska disertacija. Ljubljana: FDV.

Zupančič, Radovan (1997) Teorija izbire in realitetna terapija. *Psihološka obzorja*, 1/2, 133–145.

Žvelc, Maša, Možina, Miran, Bohak, Janko (ur.) (2011) *Psihoterapija.* Ljubljana: IPSA.